THE NATIONAL HEALTH SERVICE:
THE FIRST PHASE

The
National Health Service:
The First Phase

1948-1974 and After

BRIAN WATKIN

London
GEORGE ALLEN & UNWIN
Boston   Sydney

**British Library Cataloguing in Publication
Data**

Watkin, Brian
    The National Health Service: The First Phase
    1. Great Britain – National Health Service –
    History
    I. Title
    362.1'0941   RA395.G6

    ISBN 0–04–362025–6
    ISBN 0–04–362026–4   Pbk.

Typeset in 10/11 Plantin by Bedford Typesetters Limited
and printed in Great Britain by Unwin Brothers Limited
The Gresham Press, Old Woking, Surrey

Contents

I

A National Health Service – A New Beginning?

*The little present must not be allowed wholly to elbow the great
past out of view.*   Andrew Lang

The period covered in this book is bounded by two years, 1948 and
1974, in each of which the systems and institutions provided by the
British people to care for their health were given a new administrative
framework. In 1948 the most important changes were in the methods
of financing health care, whilst in 1974 the emphasis was more on
changes of organisation and systems of management, although there
were financial changes as well. In each case, however, there was much
continuity with what had gone before. Phrases such as 'the creation of
the National Health Service', when used in relation to the legislation
which took effect in 1948, can be justified only from a legal or administrative standpoint. The National Health Service Act of 1946 created no
new hospitals, trained no new doctors, brought no new drugs or methods
of treatment into being; these things were there already. It did not even
make available to the poor what had previously only been available to
the rich, although it made it simpler for the poor to have access to the
services they required. In 1973 the National Health Service Reorganisation Act attracted surprisingly little public discussion, and on 1 April
1974 there was no reason why any patient should notice that the Act
had come into effect. Turmoil and change there was indeed, but it was
an internal matter, involving those working in the service rather than
the community at large.

The term 'National Health Service' has been criticised because it is
said that the service is not truly national, since some parts of the country,
and some sections of society, enjoy a more generous provision of services

than others, and because it does not concern itself in the main with health, but rather with the treatment of ill health and the care of those who are sick. There may be some justice in these criticisms, although they both beg a number of questions, but it does not do to pick at slogans as if they represent a close and scientific definition of what they describe, and 'National Health Service' was essentially a slogan – calling for better organisation of health care services, and a better system of financing – which became embodied in legislation. Whether the legislation achieved these aims is a question that must be examined, but first it will be necessary to consider what those responsible for the changes of 1946–8 had in mind when they looked to a better form of organisation and system of financing and what criteria they would have been willing to accept as a basis on which their achievement could be fairly judged. Only then will it be reasonable to suggest other aims and other criteria which, with hindsight, might seem to have been preferable.

BACKGROUND

The decision to introduce a national health service must be seen not only against the background of the 1940s, with all the disruption of war and postwar impoverishment, but also against that of the 1930s, which in the postwar years remained for most people a normality to which it was hoped to return or from which it was hoped to escape. War created the opportunity to think in terms of reconstruction and to capture the imagination of a people face to face with annihilation through gestures and language which at other times might have seemed inflated and rhetorical. Churchill and Beveridge – and later Aneurin Bevan – responded in their different ways to this heightened atmosphere.

The National Health Service Act of 1946 was passed as part of the great wave of social legislation introduced by the Labour government which came into power in 1945 towards the end of the Second World War, but had the Conservatives come to power they too would have legislated for health, and the conviction that something must be done about the nation's health services had been growing among thinking people of all shades of opinion for many a year.

To consider why this should have been so we must look at Britain's health services and the health of the people in the last years of peace. During the war, health services, in common with most aspects of national life, were placed on an emergency footing. The health of the people, too, was subject to a number of exceptional influences, ranging from enemy action bringing in its train death and maiming, to the probably beneficent effects of rationing and other controls on the nutritional well-being of the population.

Because, as Professor and Mrs Jewkes have pointed out, it is usual to paint conditions before any great reform much blacker than they really were, partly in order to strengthen the case for reform and partly perhaps because it feeds our sense of the dramatic, it comes as a surprise to read in Lord Horder's preface to the popular version of the 1937 Political and Economic Planning (PEP) *Report on the British Health Services* that 'it is universally acknowledged that our Health Services are the best in the world'. This may not mean much, of course. The National Health Service has in its turn been said to be 'regarded all over the world as the most civilised achievement of modern government', albeit by the man who as Minister of Health inaugurated it, while Lord Horder, one of the most eminent doctors of his day, was, after the war, foremost among those who opposed the National Health Service Act.

Yet Lord Horder was not indulging in an uncritical panegyric, and there is evidence that his view was widely shared. The coalition government's 1944 White Paper on *A National Health Service* declared:

The record of this country in its health and medical services is a good one. The resistance of people to the wear and tear of four years of a second world war bears testimony to it. Achievements before the war – in lower mortality rates, in the gradual decline of many of the more serious diseases, in safer motherhood and healthier childhood, and generally in the prospect of a longer and safer life – all substantiate it. There is no question of having to abandon bad services and to start afresh. Reform in this field is not a matter of making good what is bad, but of making better what is good already.

Lord Horder went on indeed to speak of the 'glaring anomalies' with which the 'system' abounded, to refer to 'the unwieldiness, the overlap, the uneconomy, the lack of integration of our Health Services as they at present exist', but he was at pains to point out that lack of planning was a British characteristic, 'the price we pay for being a highly individualised society'. There were also 'parts of the machinery of our Health Services which work perfectly; some units stand out as pieces of perfect organisation and efficiency: a large general teaching hospital, a well-run cottage hospital, some of our Public Health Services, our Medical Research Council'. 'It is', he went on, 'when we come to consider the machine as a whole that both organisation and efficiency are found to be unsatisfactory.' That was in fact the main burden of the PEP Report, which spoke of the 'bewildering variety' of agencies, public and voluntary, which had been created during the previous two or three decades to work for health, and called on those concerned with British health services to look at them 'less as a mass of separate expedients, and more as a whole in relation to the national life'. The PEP Report represented an impassioned plea for planning and co-ordination, and for the claims of prevention over the cure of established disease.

PEP estimated that in 1937 about 4·2 per cent of the national income was spent on medical care, but showed a sophisticated awareness that health services were by no means the only factor influencing the health of the population, and that at times other factors, such as housing, nutrition and standards of living generally, might be more important. Emphasising that it was not possible to measure how far any improvement in health that had taken place over the years was due to the health services, the Report none the less recorded the changes that had occurred since the turn of the century and argued that some of the improvement must be due to health services.

There was, inevitably, a problem of definition. What were health services? In this work we shall evade the issue by allowing the Act of 1946 to, in effect, define health services for us, but the PEP Report suggested it was important 'to outgrow the attitude of confining the term health services to what are really sickness services'.

> The really essential health services of the nation are the making available of ample safe fresh milk to all who need it, the cheapening of other dairy produce, fruit and vegetables, new accommodation to replace slums and relieve overcrowding, green belt schemes, playing fields, youth hostels and physical education, social insurances which relieve the burden of anxiety on the family and advances in employment policy which improve security of tenure or conditions of work and, finally, education in healthy living through training and propaganda.

Health in the 1930s
So how healthy was Britain in the 1930s? Drawing on the PEP Report and other sources we can see that the 1930s were a decade in which much had already been achieved. Economically the decade was one characterised at first by crises and recession, followed by recovery as most of the nations of Europe began, reluctantly or eagerly as the case may be, to prepare for war. The folklore of the period is dominated by the massive unemployment figures of the early years and by the great distress of the depressed areas where unemployment involved whole communities, but taking the country as a whole it is true to say that throughout the 1930s the cost of living either held steady or in some years actually fell, and for those who stayed in employment wage increases ensured that they enjoyed a small but perceptible rise in their standard of living.

Some of what had already been achieved in health terms was reflected in the structure of the population, which at the 1931 census numbered, in England and Wales, just under 40 million, a 23 per cent increase since the turn of the century in spite of a fall in the birth rate from 28·5 to 15·1 per 1,000 population. Obviously fewer deaths were occurring. The crude death rate per 1,000 population had shown fairly steady improvement since it fell below 20 for the first time in 1881. In 1908 it fell below 15 for the first time and only the 1918 influenza epidemic lifted it above that figure. In 1938, the last full year of peace, it was 11·6, and it was still 11·6 at the beginning of the 1970s, although there had in fact been some small further improvement, as is revealed if the figures are standardised for age and sex.

An effect of the falling death rate was the growing number of elderly people. The natural span of life had not lengthened significantly, but the average man or woman had a better chance of reaching old age, as the improvement in the death rates was marked at all ages between one week and 75 years for men, 80 for women. At the 1931 census, 7·4 per cent of the population was over 65, compared with only 4·6 per cent in 1901. By the 1970s the percentage was 13·3, a further dramatic change, while in contrast the proportion of children under 15 – around 24 per cent – was much the same as it had been in the 1930s.

Infants under one year, a particularly vulnerable group, shared in the general improvement in mortality in the early decades of the twentieth century. In 1938 the death rate of infants per 1,000 live births was 53 in England and Wales (although it was 70 in Scotland and 75 in Northern Ireland). Again the improvement had been steady since the turn of the century, with the rate falling below 100 for the first time in 1912. None the less the figure was still high by more recent standards; in the 1970s a figure of 17·5 per 1,000 was not regarded with complacency. One-quarter of all infant deaths occurred within the first two days of life – the twentieth century had by 1938 seen little improvement in mortality during the first week – but for all who survived that perilous week the risk of death had been very much reduced. It was among young adults that it had proved most difficult to bring about marked improvements in the death rates, and this reflected the prevalence of tuberculosis in early adult life and a high accident rate among young men.

The population we have described was therefore one in which it was becoming more common to reach old age, in which fewer children were being born but more children were reaching maturity than at any previous time. There was an unusual excess of women over men, but this largely stemmed from the carnage of the First World War and was beginning to correct itself. Meanwhile such professions as teaching and nursing were dominated by unmarried women, a situation which did not change for another two decades.

However, although the structure of the population had begun to take on modern lines, the pattern of disease experienced by this population was quite different from that which came to prevail from the 1950s onwards. Let us consider first the causes of the still relatively high infant mortality rate. Of deaths occurring in the first month of life, 70 per cent were due to prematurity or to conditions present at birth, but after the first month the main hazards to young babies were diarrhoea and infectious diseases (accounting together for 52 per cent of deaths between one month and one year), although prematurity and congenital disorders still took a substantial toll (23 per cent of deaths between one month and one year).

For children between 1 and 5, measles and pneumonia and, for girls, whooping cough, were the most serious dangers, with diphtheria also a hazard. Between 5 and 15 diphtheria was the most important single cause of death, taking boys and girls together, although accidents were responsible for more deaths among boys. In early adult life the principal cause of death was tuberculosis for both sexes, with accidents running a close second among men; in late middle age heart disease and cancer dominated the picture as they do today. In 1936, 11 per cent of deaths were certified as due to 'old age', and the existence of this group somewhat confused the analysis of deaths over the age of 70.

In the late 1930s more than 15 per cent of all deaths were due to infectious diseases of one kind or another, including tuberculosis. This was a rather higher proportion than was attributable to cancer. Yet contemporaries were pleased to note that, with the exception of influenza, mortality rates from this group of diseases had been falling, and when Lord Horder reviewed 'Old Diseases and New' in an address to the Royal Institution in 1937 his tone was cautiously optimistic. 'Influenza', he said, 'is the great outstanding plague with which Medicine has still to contend . . . *Typhoid Fever*, formerly a serious disease, both in epidemic and sporadic form, is now largely under control, as also is *Diphtheria*, though we see outbreaks of both of these diseases whenever well-known preventive measures are neglected. *Measles* and *Scarlet Fever* are still with us, but virulent epidemics of both of these are much less common than they were.'

'What of the "Great White Scourge"?' he went on. 'The great decrease in the incidence, and in the severity, of tuberculosis, witnessed during the past thirty years, has largely escaped popular attention. It is perhaps the greatest achievement of all in the control of infectious disease in this generation.' In spite of the fact that in that year more than 30,000 deaths from tuberculosis occurred in England and Wales, Lord

Horder was able to point to the fact that deaths from this cause had fallen dramatically since the turn of the century and, even though doctors still lacked a specific treatment for the disease, he was ready to predict: 'It certainly looks as though Bunyan's "Captain of the Men of Death" will be overcome in a couple of generations.'

As the PEP Report explained a few months later, 'tuberculosis is generally agreed to be a poverty disease', but Lord Horder was pleased to point out that two other diseases associated with poverty and low standards of nourishment, 'chlorosis' (iron-deficiency anaemia) and rickets, were 'fast dying out'. Of the 'new' diseases, disorders of the heart and blood vessels had become more prominent in recent years, and coronary thrombosis was apparently becoming more common. So was cancer, but this was recognised to be to a large extent at least a consequence of the changing age structure of the population. More people were surviving to the ages at which cancer was likely. There was, too, an increasing prevalence (or increasing diagnosis?) of diabetes mellitus, and a 'large increase', Lord Horder felt, in neurosis. Among the infections, chronic forms were becoming more common whilst the incidence of acute infections was falling.

Once again a modern pattern is starting to emerge, with degenerative disorders and perhaps 'diseases of civilisation' coming to the fore, but this was the view of an exceptionally well-informed medical man. To the man in the street the shadow of such diseases as diphtheria and tuberculosis still lay over the land and human life was much at the mercy of organisms against which the medical profession was ill equipped to do battle. Vaccination, immunisation and rising standards of nutrition, housing and hygiene were building on the foundations laid by the Victorian sanitary reformers who had triumphed against cholera and other water-borne diseases, and the statistics told the story of how effective such measures could be even when specific treatments for established disease did not exist.

Health services before 1948
We have said that the PEP Report fully recognised that standards of health were influenced by such factors as nutrition, housing, working conditions and the use of leisure, even though it was not practicable to bring the whole life of the community within the compass of a review of health services. Similarly, as we turn to examine the health services as they were in the decade before the inauguration of the National Health Service, and to glance briefly at their origins, it is worth noting that death rates in Britain were falling even before the Victorians enacted the legislation which brought such plagues as cholera and typhoid fever firmly under control. This was an expression of the rising standards of

living which were experienced, in greater or lesser degree, by all classes as a result first of improvements in agriculture and later of the Industrial Revolution and the accompanying improvements in transport and trade. We shall, however, go no further back than 1848 in briefly tracing the origins of those services which in the years immediately after the Second World War were in the forefront of the battle against disease, disability and premature death.

The Public Health Act of 1848 was a major landmark because it signified the first clear acceptance by the state of responsibility for promoting the health of the people, and because it established at local level the post of medical officer of health, armed with statutory powers to combat local inertia and vested interests. The value of such appointments had already been demonstrated in Liverpool and London under local Acts, but the 1848 Act empowered local boards of health throughout the land to follow this example. By 1936, when public health legislation was codified in a new Public Health Act, the medical officers of health had under their direction a wide range of services concerned with the control of infectious diseases, the prevention of environmental hazards to health, the provision of school health services, and the provision, either directly or through voluntary agencies, of district nursing and midwifery services. They also controlled a network of public hospitals.

By 1939 there were in England and Wales about 3,000 hospitals providing about 500,000 beds. These included about 1,000 voluntary hospitals, providing roughly 100,000 beds, and some 2,000 local authority hospitals providing the remaining 400,000 beds. About half the local authority beds (i.e. 200,000 or 40 per cent of the total number of hospital beds) were in the 300 or so hospitals for the mentally ill and mentally handicapped. Of the 1,000 voluntary hospitals, about one-third specialised in a particular branch of medicine, such as the care and treatment of children, obstetrics and gynaecology, diseases of the eye, orthopaedics, etc. Of the remaining 700 general hospitals in the voluntary sector, only 75 had more than 200 beds and more than 500 had fewer than 100 beds. This group included numerous cottage hospitals with perhaps a dozen to 30 beds, medically staffed by local general practitioners. Where in the larger voluntary hospitals consultants and specialists had charge of beds, they were usually unpaid, and relied for their living on the fees paid by private patients – although it was recognised that an appointment to the staff of a voluntary hospital conferred a status that was valuable in building up a private practice.

The voluntary hospitals were developing rapidly at this time. Between 1921 and 1938 their bed numbers grew from 56,550 to 87,235, an increase of 54 per cent. The corresponding increase in the public sector (excluding hospitals for the mentally ill and handicapped) was from 172,006 to 175,868, or just over 2 per cent. This differential growth had the effect of increasing the proportion of beds for the physically ill provided by the voluntary sector from 24 per cent in 1921 to 33 per cent in 1938. The voluntary hospitals were dependent for money mainly on their endowments, subscriptions and donations – including the proceeds of such ventures as 'flag days' – and on a variety of contributory schemes by which a working man could purchase the assurance of hospital care for himself and his family for a few pence a week. Clearly during the 1930s money was flowing into the coffers of the voluntary hospitals to finance the substantial expansion we have noted. The total income of the voluntary hospitals rose steadily and until 1938 kept well ahead of total expenditure. In 1938 the system as a whole showed a deficit (although of course in earlier years individual hospitals had been in difficulties), but wartime brought government subsidies and renewed prosperity. The 1930s also saw significant growth in the number of medical school places and in the numbers of nurses being trained by the voluntary hospitals – in both cases keeping somewhat ahead of the rate of increase of the population.

The local authority hospitals included many former Poor Law infirmaries which the local authorities had inherited when the boards of guardians were disbanded in 1929, together with a network of infectious diseases hospitals established under nineteenth-century sanitary legislation. Some of the former Poor Law infirmaries were equipped and staffed at a standard equal to that of the better voluntary hospitals and were doing similar work, but on the whole the local authority hospitals were heavily biased towards the care of the elderly and chronically sick, and standards were variable. In 1929 the local authorities had been empowered to establish and run general hospitals but by 1939 only about half of them had made use of these powers. The London County Council, which had inherited the already extensive hospital system of the Metropolitan Asylums Board, was a notable exception. By the time the National Health Service was launched, the LCC had about 100 hospitals, with 70,000 beds, many of them staffed and equipped to a high standard. They included the Hammersmith Hospital, the home from 1935 onwards of the British Postgraduate Medical School. More than the voluntary hospitals, the local authority hospitals had been held back in the 1930s by the difficulties through which the national economy was passing, and their relatively slow rate of expansion was the result.

By the outbreak of war, about half the population were covered for hospital inpatient and outpatient care by the multitude of hospital contributory schemes; all could, of course, claim admission in case of need to a public hospital, where patients were expected to pay according to their means. In addition, hospital outpatient departments were being used on a large scale as an alternative to general practitioner care by the dependents of working men who were themselves covered for general medical services by National Health Insurance and by others who were not covered by the scheme.

Thus, before the war the poor at least could generally obtain medical care, and if necessary admission to a hospital, without charge, or at a very modest charge, at the time of use. There were gaps in provision, but often they were closed informally by doctors who worked on the 'Robin Hood' principle, charging their middle-class patients more than the economic rate for their services so as to offset the losses they incurred in caring for the poor at reduced fees or no fees at all. This may have been hard on the middle classes, for if they were above the income limit for National Health Insurance they for the most part had to meet their doctor's and hospital bills at the time they were incurred. Aneurin Bevan made great play in the House of Commons on what he was doing for the middle classes in introducing the National Health Service, but it may be that he was overstating the case. Professor and Mrs Jewkes have said it is 'curious' that private health insurance had not developed to any great extent in Britain before the war. This would indeed be curious if the burden of medical and hospital bills were as crushing as Bevan suggested, but the explanation may be that in an era when surgical operations were relatively straightforward, hospital staff were ill paid and worked long hours, and the middle classes were still comparatively prosperous, private health insurance had not developed because there was no great demand for it.

Many criticisms of existing health services were current during the 1930s, and the PEP Report embodied some of them. There was often thought to be a shortage of hospital beds, but there was a notable absence of criteria on which to judge how many there ought to be. Much the same could be said of the alleged shortages of doctors, nurses and other staff and facilities. A recurring theme was the lack of co-ordination between the public and voluntary hospitals and between individual hospitals. Again it was not always clear what kind of co-ordination was felt to be required, but the 1944 White Paper (see below) criticised the fact that it was possible for one hospital to have a long waiting list for admission, whilst another nearby had empty beds, and that two hospitals in the same area might both be providing specialist units which could with advantage be combined into one.

On the other hand, efforts to promote co-ordination and co-operation were not lacking. The King Edward's Hospital Fund for London had been working since 1896 to promote co-operation and some standardisation of administrative and accounting procedures among the voluntary hospitals of the metropolis, and in 1939 the Nuffield Provincial Hospitals Trust was created to promote, in the words of the trust deed:

> the co-ordination on a regional basis of hospital and ancillary medical services throughout the Provinces and the making of financial provision for the creation carrying on or extension of such hospital and ancillary medical services as in the opinion of the Governing Trustees are necessary for such co-ordination.

By 1941 the Trust had devised a plan to establish a series of regional and divisional advisory councils, bringing together representatives from both local authority and voluntary hospitals. Several of these councils had been set up by the time the government asked the Trust to suspend action so as to avoid any potential conflict with their own plans for the future organisation of the hospital service.

During the war the Trust co-operated with the Ministry of Health in carrying out a series of regional hospital surveys designed to discover just what hospitals Britain had and what state they were in. The surveys provided evidence of the extent to which voluntary and local authority hospitals were entering into arrangements to co-ordinate their work and to avoid unnecessary duplication of expensive facilities. Even before the war joint planning and consultative committees had been set up in many areas, and in Birmingham, Liverpool and Manchester voluntary and local authority hospitals had gone a long way towards providing a co-ordinated service for the population as a whole. However, even in the course of putting forward proposals for closer relationships between the twenty or so voluntary hospitals in the Liverpool area, the Liverpool Hospitals Commission declared: 'Our inquiries have satisfied us that the service has been brought to a very high degree of excellence; and furthermore, that its present excellence is attributable very largely to the way in which it has grown up, and the freedom and flexibility of its organisation.' It was an arguable point of view.

EARLY PROPOSALS

The theme of co-ordination appeared early in the discussions and proposals which were eventually issued in the National Health Service Act of 1946. The Royal Commission on the Poor Laws which reported in 1909 – and here we are referring to the majority report – were moved by evidence which indicted ill health as a chief cause of poverty, to devise a scheme for the better co-ordination of the various agencies offering medical services to the poor. The scheme included provision for bringing about closer co-operation between the voluntary hospitals and those supported by the rates, but it did not envisage that hospitals or general practitioners should give their services free of charge to any except the destitute. The working classes should be encouraged to subscribe to a network of provident dispensaries which would offer a choice of doctors whose services would be available for a modest fee, and institutional treatment, on the recommendation of a doctor, for those who needed it. The Commissioners had reservations about making medical supervision 'from the cradle to the grave' too readily available. 'A race of hypochondriacs might be as useless to the State as a race of any other degenerates. Good health is no doubt a matter of the greatest importance to all, but it is not the sole aim in life, and it is possible to exaggerate the part it plays in the attainment of human welfare.'

The 1911 National Insurance Act provided for general medical services to be available to manual workers and other employees earning less than £160 a year on payment of a weekly contribution of fourpence, to which the employer added threepence, and the State a further twopence. This scheme did not include consultant or hospital care and thus did not touch the question of the co-ordination of the voluntary and public hospitals. In 1918, the Labour Party published a report entitled *The Organisation of the Preventive and Curative Medical Services and Hospital and Laboratory Systems under a Ministry of Health*. This urged the integration of curative and preventive services, the creation of a free national health service staffed mainly by full-time salaried doctors, and a nationwide network of health centres. The following year a Ministry of Health was created and Dr Christopher Addison, a medical doctor, was appointed Minister. One of his first acts was to set up a Consultative Council on Medical and Allied Services under the chairmanship of Sir Bertrand Dawson – or Lord Dawson of Penn as he became in April 1920. All but two or three members of the Council were medically qualified, and they included Dr H. G. Dain, later to lead the British Medical Association in opposition to the National Health Service Act of 1946. In 1920 the Council published an Interim Report – the only one they ever published. The Report, which quickly became known as the Dawson Report, and has been described as 'the parent of all regional schemes of health services', urged that preventive and curative health services should be integrated and based on a network of primary and secondary health centres. The secondary health centres would be based on existing general hospitals, and these in turn would be brought into relationship with the teaching hospitals. Health services would be administered by largely elected health authorities, each of which would appoint a principal medical officer as the administrative head, and responsible to him would be the professional heads of various services, such as the principal dental officer, principal matron, etc. The Dawson

Report left open the question of how health services were to be paid for, but pronounced firmly against whole-time salaried service for doctors, which would tend, it suggested, 'to discourage initiative, to diminish the sense of responsibility, and to encourage mediocrity'.

In 1926 a Royal Commission on National Health Insurance recommended that the 1911 scheme should be extended to cover contributors' dependents, and that benefits should be extended to include dental and ophthalmic treatment, although not inpatient care in hospital. Political and administrative difficulties stood in the way of the kind of extensions envisaged by the Royal Commission and only minor amendments were made to the scheme as a result of their deliberations. By 1939 National Health Insurance covered about half the population, with an income limit of £250 a year, which at the beginning of the Second World War was raised to £420.

In 1929 the British Medical Association, who initially had welcomed the Dawson Report, produced their own *Proposals for a General Medical Service for the Nation*, subsequently revised by Dr Charles Hill, then deputy secretary – later, during the Association's postwar confrontation with Aneurin Bevan, secretary – and republished in 1938 as *A General Medical Service for the Nation*. The four basic principles of the Association's scheme were:

(1) That the system of medical services should be directed to the achievement of positive health and the prevention of disease no less than to the relief of sickness.
(2) That there should be provided for every individual the services of a general practitioner or family doctor of his own choice.
(3) That consultants and specialists, laboratory services, and all necessary auxiliary services, together with institutional provision when required, should be available for the individual patient, normally through the agency of the family doctor.
(4) That the several parts of the complete medical service should be closely co-ordinated and developed by the application of a planned national health policy.

The BMA envisaged the extension of National Health Insurance to cover all those with incomes below £250 a year, but not to provide for hospital and consultant services. Voluntary and local authority hospitals would continue to be financed in the traditional ways, but there would be regional co-ordinating machinery of the kind also suggested in 1937 by the Voluntary Hospitals Commission in the Sankey Report. Payment of voluntary hospital consultants was proposed in all cases in which the hospital itself received payment, either directly, from a local authority, or through a contributory scheme.

In 1942 there was published the Interim Report of the Medical Planning Commission, which had been set up by the BMA in collaboration with the Royal College of Physicians, the Royal College of Surgeons, and other medical bodies. This Report proposed extensions of the National Health Insurance scheme which would have brought 90 per cent of the population within its ambit, leaving the remaining 10 per cent to be catered for by private practice. General practitioners should continue to be paid capitation fees, but there should also be a basic salary and separate fees for work not covered by the capitation fees – a minority of the Commission advocated a salaried service. Doctors should practise in groups, preferably from health centres provided by the local authority and furnished with the services of midwives, district nurses and health visitors. The Report did not advocate the abolition of the doctor's right to buy or sell his practice, but agreed that this might eventually come about. Regional councils would be responsible for the supervision of local health services and the co-ordination of the work of voluntary and local authority hospitals, which should be persuaded to work together in groups without change of ownership. Central co-ordination and supervision of health services would be through a government department or public corporation responsible, through a minister, to Parliament. Grants in aid should be paid to the voluntary hospitals from Exchequer funds, so as to enable them, *inter alia*, to pay part-time salaries to their consultants and specialists and thus promote a more even distribution of consultant services over the country as a whole. As long as voluntary hospital consultants were not paid they could only set up in practice in districts well supplied with potential private patients.

BEVERIDGE AND AFTER

Later the same year, the Beveridge Report on Social Insurance and Allied Services was published, with its proposal that after the war there should be an all-out attack on the 'five giants' of Want, Disease, Ignorance, Squalor and Idleness. A comprehensive health and rehabilitation service should be made available to every citizen on the basis of need, irrespective of means or the payment of insurance contributions. Small charges might be made, but they should not be such as to stand as a barrier between the citizen and the service he required. Such a service would eventually pay for itself by making the nation fitter and more productive.

Meanwhile, world events had made their own contribution to the continuing discussion of the future organisation of Britain's health services. As it became obvious during the late 1930s that Britain faced the prospect of a war in which the civilian population would be exposed to attack from the air on a scale never before experienced, plans were laid to ensure that hospital beds could be made available to receive and treat large numbers of casualties. Under the Emergency Medical Service administered by the Ministry of Health, all existing hospital accommodation was pooled, and about 50,000 extra beds were provided in the form of hutted extensions. In addition, extra operating theatres and other facilities were provided at a number of hospitals, including some mental hospitals whose patients were transferred elsewhere for the duration of the war. Each hospital was expected not only to treat casualties from its own area but also to receive casualties and other patients from elsewhere when required to do so. The ministry took powers to determine the type of work for which each hospital could best be used, and regional hospital officers were appointed to plan, co-ordinate and exercise general control. In the counties and county boroughs the medical officers of health acted as the agents of the regional hospital officers. Doctors were recruited into the Emergency Medical Service on a salaried basis to work in any hospitals that needed them, and a Civil Nursing Reserve was recruited.

The scale of preparations reflected the alarming estimates of the likely numbers of air-raid casualties that were being made in the immediate prewar period, and in the event many voluntary hospitals were paid considerable sums of government money to maintain empty beds for the reception of casualties who never arrived. Others found themselves treating military rather than civilian patients. But the exercise provided valuable experience in the co-ordination of hospital services on a national scale, although it was achieved without any transfer of ownership, and it revealed to many teaching and voluntary hospital doctors variations in standards of which they had not been aware before.

Following publication of the Beveridge Report, the coalition government announced acceptance of the principle of a national health service, and the Minister of Health, Ernest Brown, opened discussions with the voluntary hospitals, the local authorities, the doctors, and other interests. Brown put forward proposals for a service that would be administered by the local authorities – although the voluntary hospitals would retain their independence – and in which general practitioners would be salaried. These proposals were not well received by the doctors and were abandoned when, at the end of 1943, Brown was succeeded as Minister by H. U. Willink.

White Paper on a National Health Service
After further discussions the government published, in February 1944,

a White Paper on a National Health Service. The White Paper made county and county borough councils responsible for primary and preventive health services and proposed joint authorities of county and county borough councils to control the municipal hospitals and to make contractual arrangements with the voluntary hospitals for the use of their facilities. Both types of hospital would receive government subsidies and the service would be financed by a combination of general taxation, local rates, and national insurance contributions. Consultants and specialists working in hospitals would be paid, and general practitioners would be given the choice of salaried service or payment by capitation fees; unless they worked in health centres owned by the local authority, in which case they would be salaried. Access to services would be on the basis of need and not ability to pay. The government, the White Paper said, wanted 'to ensure that in future every man and woman and child can rely on getting all the advice and treatment and care which they may need in matters of personal health; that what they get shall be the best medical and other facilities available'. In the House of Commons Willink described the four basic principles of the plan as:

(1) the provision of a comprehensive service, available to all;
(2) freedom for both doctors and patients to take part in the service or not as they wished;
(3) democratic control through Parliament and the elected local authorities;
(4) machinery to ensure that the views of the professions were taken into account in the development of the service.

The last point referred to the proposal that the minister would be advised by a Central Health Services Council, and each joint authority would have a Local Health Services Council to advise it.

In a postal poll on the White Paper proposals conducted by the British Medical Association, general practitioners came out strongly against the scheme, whilst consultants and specialists were more receptive. There was strong opposition to the administration of the health service by local authorities, and in the extension of the scheme to the entire population – as distinct from the 90 per cent who would have been covered in the proposals of the Medical Planning Commission – some doctors detected a threat to the continuance of private practice. Both the BMA and the British Hospital Association, representing the voluntary hospitals, feared for the future independence of the voluntary hospitals, while the major local authorities were suspicious of the new joint authorities and wanted them restricted to planning, with no executive responsibilities. The general public on the whole welcomed the proposals, and in particular the promise that the service would be free at the time of use.

Bevan and the doctors

By early 1945, following yet more discussions, Willink was ready to draft a Bill, but before the Bill could be introduced a general election had brought a Labour government to power and Aneurin Bevan to the Ministry of Health. Bevan quickly came to the conclusion that Willink had conceded too much to vested interests and that his scheme would not be workable. He pointedly avoided picking up discussions with the doctors, local authorities and other interests where Willink had left off. As a critic of the coalition government he had expressed strong opposition to the erosion of the sovereignty of Parliament which he felt to be implied by the willingness of ministers to negotiate, as distinct from consult, with outside bodies. Willink, he held, had come dangerously near negotiation.

In January 1946 Bevan outlined his proposals to the Council of the British Medical Association; two months later the publication of a White Paper embodying them was followed rapidly by the first reading of the National Health Service Bill. Clause 1 of the Bill stated:

(1) It shall be the duty of the Minister of Health to promote the establishment in England and Wales of a comprehensive health service designed to secure improvement in the physical and mental health of the people of England and Wales and the prevention, diagnosis and treatment of illness, and for that purpose to provide or secure the effective provision of services in accordance with the following provisions of this Act.

(2) The services so provided shall be free of charge, except where any provision of this Act expressly provides for the making and recovery of charges.

Bevan took these statements seriously and insisted that as such a duty was to be laid on the minister, he must have the power to discharge it. This meant, among other things, that the hospitals must be vested in the minister. Only by nationalisation of both the voluntary and local authority hospitals could effective co-ordination be achieved and a planned hospital service developed from the existing patchwork. Only by nationalisation could the provincial hospitals be enabled to pay consultants the salaries and provide them with the facilities that would draw them out of the big cities and ensure a more even distribution of their services. If the minister was to 'promote the establishment . . . of a comprehensive health service' he must, in Bevan's view, have the means of providing such a service in his own hand. 'How', he asked, 'can the State enter into contract with a citizen to render service through an autonomous body ?' Willink's plan was 'a hopelessly impracticable compromise based not upon functional considerations but merely a desire to conciliate conflicting interests'.

The Bill was fought fiercely in Parliament and outside by the doctors. The ostensible grounds on which the Conservative Opposition opposed the Bill were outlined in a motion, put down during the second reading, which predicted a loss of independence for the general practitioner and criticised the nationalisation of the hospitals. An Opposition amendment to the third reading elaborated these objections: the Bill was one 'which discourages voluntary effort and association; mutilates the structure of local government; dangerously increases ministerial power and patronage; appropriates trust funds and benefactions in contempt of the wishes of donors and subscribers; and undermines the freedom and independence of the medical profession to the detriment of the nation'.

Bevan had little difficulty in answering these attacks. Experience with the Emergency Medical Service had shown how unsuitable were local authority areas for hospital purposes, and he had little patience with voluntarism. 'It is repugnant to a civilized community', he said, 'for hospitals to have to rely upon private charity. . . . I have always felt a shudder of repulsion when I have seen nurses and sisters who ought to be at their work, and students who ought to be at theirs, going about the streets collecting money for the hospitals.' The real reason for the bitterness of the critics, he argued, 'is because this is taking away from them one of their chief sources of social and political patronage. It is notorious in the world of medicine that doctors, first-class people, first-class surgeons, gynaecologists and general physicians have from time to time to desert the practice of their profession in order to seduce millionaires to provide money for teaching medicine.' In fact he was convinced that those who were actually running the voluntary hospitals were secretly delighted at the prospect of being relieved of financial worry.

The opposition outside Parliament – where Labour had in any case an almost two-to-one majority – was a different matter. The British Medical Association represented 75–80 per cent of all practising doctors. Medicine is, however, a highly individualistic profession and doctors do not willingly relinquish power to representatives to speak on their behalf. The BMA constitution included, in the words of the Webbs, 'all the devices of advanced democracy' to ensure that the leadership continued to reflect the wishes of the members at large, and to guard against the concentration of power in the hands of the officers. This made the Association a difficult body to consult with – let alone negotiate – even when the doctors were not trying to be difficult. A Council of some seventy members were answerable to the Representative Body, which met annually unless specially called together, and which could make binding decisions only by a two-thirds majority. The Representative Body consisted of some 300 representatives. A large number of committees supervised the day-to-day work of the Association and the activities of the full-time officers. The constitution provided for important issues to be referred to the entire membership by means of plebiscites. BMA leaders were often left with astonishingly little room to manoeuvre by decisions taken in the heat of the moment and reversible only by procedures which were cumbersome in the extreme. At times their difficulties were compounded by the fact that the *British Medical Journal,* the official organ of the Association, enjoyed full editorial freedom, and the editor was a power in his own right.

The BMA's intransigence was difficult to explain if account were taken only of the proposals which were the ostensible ground of debate. The Medical Planning Commission had advocated that general practitioners should be paid a basic salary, plus capitation fees, but this proposal from Bevan was considered to be quite unacceptable. The Medical Planning Commission were prepared to contemplate the abolition of the right to buy and sell doctors' practices, but this was anathema to the BMA when it was suggested by a Labour government.

An explanation was offered by David Eccles (later Lord Eccles), speaking in the House of Commons in February 1948.

I do not think we can understand why the opposition of the doctors to the Minister has increased unless we see the Minister's recent obstinacy as one of a series of blows delivered by this Government against the middle class. Houses are not to be built for sale; the purchasing power of professional incomes goes steadily down; the basic petrol ration is abolished; university seats in this House are to disappear; and now there is talk of a capital levy which will hit those people for whom the Secretary of State for War does not care a 'tinker's cuss'. All this looks like a concerted attack on the middle class.

Looking at it from such a viewpoint, it could be said that the government were waging not a conventional, but a guerrilla war against the propertied class – with whom the middle class as a whole tended to identify – and in this type of war opportunities to stand and fight a pitched battle were few. The doctors, however, represented a segment of the middle class which was in a position to fight a pitched battle with the government, and it is possible that the resentment they felt, as members of the middle class, at the government's general line, coloured and distorted their perceptions of what the government were proposing to do in the field of health. This is rather different from the usual portrayal of the doctors as a pressure group protecting narrowly defined sectional interests, but it helps to explain the anomaly of a profession opposing measures which had in the past been discussed without heat when put forward by leading members of that profession.

Bevan was not unnerved by the doctors' combative mood both before and after the passage of the Act. He believed that the Act, when it came into force, would offer advantages not only to the majority of doctors, but also to the middle class as a whole. 'There is nothing', he said, speaking in the same debate as Eccles, 'that destroys the family budget of the professional worker more than heavy hospital bills and doctors' bills . . . I know of middle-class families who are mortgaging their future and their children's future because of heavy surgeons' bills and doctors' bills.'

In February 1948 Bevan moved in the House a motion reaffirming support for the Act and inviting the House to express satisfaction 'that the conditions under which all the professions concerned are invited to participate are generous and fully in accord with their traditional freedom and dignity'. Once again Bevan was asserting his belief that Parliament was the correct forum in which to debate great issues before the nation, and he used the occasion to set out the concessions he had made to medical opinion, and the extent to which he had stretched constitutional convention in entering into what might reasonably be termed negotiations with the doctors while the Bill was going through Parliament. What more could the doctors ask for? They were so well protected that it was in his mind that perhaps patients were not protected enough. Some of the further concessions the doctors were seeking to extract from him – such as a right of appeal to the High Court from the minister's decision to dispense with a doctor's services – they would one day thank him for refusing, for a court hearing would involve publicity that would damage a doctor's reputation whether or not his appeal was upheld.

None the less, at the crucial moment when influential members of the BMA were beginning to see that they had got themselves in an impossible position, he offered a further concession. He had repeatedly declared it was not his intention to introduce a fully salaried service, but the doctors had not believed him. Now he would introduce in Parliament an amending Bill to make it impossible to introduce a fully salaried service without further legislation. Once again Bevan's insistence on the sovereignty of Parliament is the key to an understanding of his readiness to make such a concession, even though in common with most Socialists of his day he believed a salaried service was the best way of providing medical care. 'There is all the difference in the world between plucking fruit when it is ripe and plucking it when it is green', he had explained at an earlier stage. What Parliament had enacted, Parliament could, when the fruit ripened, undoubtedly repeal, and why should a good democrat object to having to go back to the forum of the people rather than be able to proceed by ministerial fiat?

The amending Bill offered the BMA leadership the chance to save face. It was by no means a climb-down, although that was how the *Economist* saw it. Publicly the doctors made a tally of the concessions they had wrung from the minister, but many years later Dr Talbot Rogers, who was a member of the profession's negotiating committee throughout this period, admitted he had come to the conclusion that Bevan 'knew all along what he wanted and the concessions he was willing to make in order to get it'.

To retire with dignity the BMA leaders had to cut some procedural corners in dealing with their own membership. A secret meeting of the Council on 15 April ordered a new plebiscite of the membership, although there were some who felt a further meeting of the Representative Body should have been called. Had this been done there was the risk that those who had become entrenched in opposition to the Act on any terms would once more have carried all before them. Ever before the BMA leaders was the spectre of the débâcle that had followed negotiations with Lloyd George over the National Insurance scheme thirty-five years before. Then the leaders had fought to the bitter end, but had been deserted by their troops, and the BMA hardly survived the discredit.

The plebiscite revealed that a majority of doctors still disapproved of the Act, but many had changed their minds, and the figures made it clear that enough doctors would accept service under the Act to make it workable. The Council therefore called a special meeting of the Representative Body for 28 May and placed before it a resolution recommending that as long as the minister was willing to continue negotiations on the amending Act, doctors should join the new service. By the time the Representative Body met, doctors were already flocking to sign the forms sent out by the Ministry of Health. The Representative Body passed the Council's resolutions; later claims for an inquiry as to how the profession had been betrayed were brushed aside. What all but the diehards realised was that a massive humiliation had been narrowly averted, and it would have served no purpose to rake over the ashes. The National Health Service therefore started on time, as the minister said it would, and his refusal to make contingency plans for postponement or emergency measures should the doctors refuse to participate was shown to be based on well-founded confidence. On 5 July 1948 the newly appointed regional hospital boards and hospital management committees assumed responsibility for the great majority of the nation's hospitals, the population flocked to register for general medical services, and in many overseas countries observers prepared to watch the progress of a service which Bevan declared would soon be 'the envy of the world'.

2

Supply and Demand – the Bottomless Pit

*When you can measure what you are speaking about and express
it in numbers, you know something about it, but when you cannot
measure it, when you cannot express it in numbers, your knowledge
is of a meagre and unsatisfactory kind.*   Lord Kelvin

The National Health Service Act which came into force on 5 July 1948
laid on the Minister of Health the duty to promote the establishment
of a comprehensive health service and vested in the minister the great
majority of both the voluntary and local authority hospitals then in
existence. About 200 voluntary hospitals were 'disclaimed' by the
minister, as the Act allowed if he considered they were not required to
enable him to fulfil his statutory obligations; these were mostly small
hospitals maintained by religious communities or for limited sections of
the population. The larger among them included the Royal Masonic
Hospital, the Manor House Hospital, maintained by the trade union
movement for its members, the Retreat at York, and St Andrew's
Hospital, Northampton. On the other hand, the Great Western Railway
Welfare Society handed over to the minister a substantial health centre
building and a small hospital in Swindon which had been provided for
railwaymen and their dependants.

THE ACT AND ITS PROVISIONS

Hospital authorities
The basic provisions affecting the hospitals were set out in Part II of
the Act. The country was divided into regions and a regional hospital
board (RHB), with chairman and members appointed by the minister,

established in each. Within a region hospitals were grouped under hospital management committees (HMCs), with chairmen and members appointed by the regional hospital board. Separate arrangements were made for the teaching hospitals, and each teaching hospital or group of teaching hospitals was given a board of governors (BoG), with a chairman and members appointed by the minister rather than by the regional hospital board. Financially, the teaching hospitals received their allocations directly from the Ministry of Health rather than through the regions and they dealt directly with the ministry on a wide range of matters for which hospital management committees had to go to their regional boards.

The Third Schedule to the Act prescribed that members of a regional hospital board should include:

(a) persons appointed after consultation with the university with which the provision of hospital and specialist services in the area of the Board is to be associated;

(b) persons appointed after consultation with such organisations as the Minister may recognise as representative of the medical profession in the said area or the medical profession generally;

(c) persons appointed after consultation with the local authorities in the said area; and

(d) persons appointed after consultation with such other organisations as appear to the Minister to be concerned.

It was also laid down that the original members of the board should include members appointed after consultation with voluntary hospital interests in the area, and that at least two members should have experience in mental health services. When vacancies arose the board was to be consulted about filling them.

The reference to a university in the provisions relating to membership stemmed from the fact that it was regarded as a principle that each region should be linked to a university having a medical school. This was partly why London was cut like a cake into four sectors, so that the London medical schools could be linked with four metropolitan regions extending from central London either to the coast or up to the Midlands, rather than falling all into one region, leaving other regions without any direct link with a medical school. England and Wales were originally divided into fourteen regions, Wales being one, although in deference to feelings that Wales was a nation rather than a region the regional board for Wales was known from 1964 onwards as the Welsh Hospital Board. The over-large South West Metropolitan Region was subsequently divided and the Wessex Region created, thus for the first time breaching the principle that each region should contain a university having a medical school. The breach was, however, only temporary, as in due course a medical school was established at Southampton University.

The function of RHBs was said in the Act to be 'generally to administer on behalf of the Minister the hospital and specialist services provided in their area', but this function was to be discharged 'subject to the exercise of functions by Hospital Management Committees', which were in turn enjoined to 'control and manage' their hospitals on behalf of the RHB, just as BoGs were to 'manage and control' their hospitals on behalf of the minister. In practice RHBs concentrated in the early years on the planning of services and general supervision of HMCs, while HMCs enjoyed a large measure of autonomy in the day-to-day management of their hospitals. The boundary between the responsibilities of the RHB and of HMCs was one that shifted over time and was drawn differently in different regions. Some regions from the beginning supervised their HMCs more closely, and required more decisions to be referred to region, than others. BoGs, on the other hand, cherished their greater degree of autonomy and fiercely resisted over the next twenty-five years any suggestion that they should be incorporated in the regional structure. One important difference between a BoG and an HMC was that, in the regions, senior medical staff were appointed and employed by the RHB, while BoGs appointed and employed their own.

Members of an HMC were to be appointed after consultation with the relevant local authorities, with executive councils (see below) whose areas related to the area served by the hospitals of the group, with senior medical and dental staff employed in the group, with such other organisations as seemed to the RHB to be concerned, and in the first instance with the governing body of any voluntary hospital being incorporated in the group. The provisions for constituting a BoG were quite different. Up to one-fifth of the members were to be nominated by the university with which the hospital or hospitals were associated, and up to one-fifth by the RHB. Not more than one-fifth of the members were to be nominated by the medical and dental teaching staff and the remainder by the minister after various consultations. Membership of all these boards and committees was voluntary and unpaid, except for reimbursement of expenses and loss of earnings. Members were normally appointed for three years and were eligible for reappointment.

The Act gave BoGs the responsibility of administering the endowments and trust moneys of the former voluntary teaching hospitals. Virtually all other voluntary hospital endowments were vested in the minister and used to establish a Hospital Endowments Fund, the income from which was distributed to RHBs and HMCs to spend as they saw fit on purposes approved by the minister but which would not be covered by the normal Exchequer allocation. These were the so-called 'free moneys' which were used for a variety of purposes, from staff amenities to the building, in the case of a BoG with trust moneys running into several million pounds, of a complete new hospital block for which funds were not available in the official building programme.

Local health authorities
Part III of the Act designated county and county borough councils as local health authorities (LHAs) and set out their health functions in eight sections, starting with: 'It shall be the duty of every local health authority to provide, equip, and maintain to the satisfaction of the Minister premises, which shall be called "health centres" . . .' In spite of this clear statement, few health centres were actually brought into operation until the late 1960s. The pioneer health centre had been that established at Peckham between the wars and like the primary health centres described in the Dawson Report it had placed great emphasis on recreational and 'keep fit' facilities, but this type of provision was played down in health centres established under the NHS. Improved standards of living and nutrition and the growth of alternative recreational facilities made the earlier pattern to some extent outmoded. The first NHS health centre was the William Budd Centre opened in Bristol in 1952, and this provided facilities for local authority clinics and for eleven general practitioners to hold their surgeries, supported by a staff of secretaries and nurses.

Most of the other functions laid down in the Act for local health authorities were already being discharged by them under earlier legislation, but the local authorities had of course lost their hospitals. They remained responsible for domiciliary midwifery, home nursing, health visiting, the care of mothers and young children, vaccination and immunisation, ambulance services, preventive services generally, and the provision of home help services.

Executive councils and other provisions
Part IV of the Act set out the arrangements for the general medical and dental services, pharmaceutical and supplementary (i.e. non-hospital) ophthalmic services. These were to be administered by executive councils set up for the area of each local health authority, or exceptionally for the area of two or more local health authorities. The executive council (EC) in effect replaced the old insurance committee set up under the 1911 Act, making contracts with doctors and dentists for the provision of services, keeping records, administering payments and operat-

ing the disciplinary machinery. There was little responsibility for policy making and the executive councils were essentially a device for avoiding a direct employer–employee relationship between general medical and dental practitioners and either the minister or local health authorities.

Other provisions of the Act included the creation of a Central Health Services Council, with a membership drawn mainly from the professions, to offer advice to the minister or to advise on matters referred by him. The Council worked largely through standing committees, of which the most important were the Standing Medical Advisory Committee and the Standing Nursing Advisory Committee. The Council and its committees had no part to play in the day-to-day running of the NHS but over the years produced a number of useful reports on specific topics.

SETTING UP THE NEW AUTHORITIES

As far as executive councils and local health authorities were concerned, there was substantial continuity with bodies that were already in existence before 1948. The hospital boards and committees had to be specially created. Once the RHBs were in existence – and the first RHB to meet was Sheffield RHB, in July 1947 – a first task was to draw up schemes for submission to the minister for the grouping of hospitals under HMCs. Within the fourteen original regions were created 388 hospital groups. Just as the regions varied in size and population, from the Oxford Region with 1·5 million population to the South West Metropolitan Region with 4·5 million population, so did the hospital groups vary. Some seventy groups comprised merely one large hospital – usually a mental illness or mental handicap hospital – while a typical general group would be based on a county town and embrace a former voluntary and a former municipal general hospital of some size together with perhaps half a dozen smaller hospitals or hospitals for the chronic sick or aged, and possibly a sanatorium or an eye hospital. Neither regional boundaries nor the catchment areas of hospital groups took any cognisance of local authority boundaries (and hence of executive council areas), but as far as the referral of patients by general practitioners, and their treatment, was concerned the boundaries had no significance. Patients could be referred as doctors saw fit and in some parts of the country there was considerable flow across regional boundaries.

The incorporation of the hospitals into groups was not achieved without heartburning among those who had previously been associated with them. Administrators and other senior officers who had served voluntary or local authority hospitals now had to work side by side for the same employer and were in competition for chief officer posts with the new HMCs. Widely varying patterns of administration and relationships between officers had to be accommodated within the same organisation. (Further discussion of these aspects will be postponed until Chapter 7.) A sense of the group as an entity with an identity of its own, distinct from that of the constituent hospitals, developed in some places faster than elsewhere, but nowhere did it happen overnight. As with most reorganisations there were those who after many years still looked back longingly to a state of affairs that had passed away.

THE COST OF THE NATIONAL HEALTH SERVICE

However, the immediate problems of the new health service were financial rather than in the spheres of organisation and morale. The phrase 'a noble ideal' has often been used to describe the NHS. At times it has been used to convey the speaker's belief that it was all very well as an ideal to offer the people a comprehensive health service free at the time of use, but that it would not work in practice, and the nation could not possibly afford it. This view gained ground in many quarters when it became clear soon after the inauguration of the NHS that the original estimates of what it would cost were somewhat optimistic. Beveridge in 1942 incorporated in his Report the estimate of the Government Actuary that a comprehensive health service for Great Britain might cost annually about £170 million. He took the view also that further development of the service would be offset by the fall in demand which would take place once the original backlog of need had been wiped out and the population became healthier as a result of better medical care, so that costs would not rise in subsequent years and the £170 million which would suffice in the immediate postwar period would still be enough twenty years later – give or take whatever allowance was necessary for changes in the value of money and price levels generally.

The 1944 White Paper estimated the cost for England and Wales alone as £132 million, with a further £6 million to be provided from the voluntary hospitals' own resources under the plan then envisaged which stopped short of nationalising the voluntary hospitals. The financial memorandum accompanying the 1946 National Health Service Bill suggested the measure would involve annual expenditure in England and Wales of about £152 million, offset to some extent by contributions from local authorities, the national insurance fund, amenity bed and other charges, so that the net cost to the Exchequer would be no more than £110 million. This was not far removed from the Beveridge estimate, since to the gross cost for England and Wales must be added, say, £19 million for Scotland, making a total for Great Britain of £171 million (Beveridge – £170 million). However, by April 1948 rising prices obliged the Minister of Health, Aneurin Bevan, to offer the House of Commons an estimate of £230 million at current prices, although he told Hugh Dalton, Chancellor of the Exchequer, that of course the figure was bound to be guesswork. The actual cost would depend on how people behaved when the service became available, and the only way to discover this would be to wait and see what happened.

In the event, Parliament was asked to vote £132·4 million to see the NHS through its first nine months from 5 July 1948 to the end of the government's accounting year on 31 March 1949. This was equivalent to about £176 million for a full year, but supplementary estimates had to be introduced and Parliament asked to vote an additional £52·8 million, giving a total for the nine months of £185·2 million, of which £179·2 million was actually spent, equivalent to nearly £240 million for a full year. This was of course the net cost to the Exchequer. The gross cost for the first nine months was well over £240 million, but this was offset by contributions from local authority rates, the National Insurance Fund, and other sources, amounting to just over £62 million.

So the picture was already beginning to look alarming. For the first full year of the service, 1949/50, the original estimate of the net cost to the Exchequer was £228·4 million, but again supplementary estimates had to be introduced and expenditure during the year turned out at £305·2 million. The estimate for the following year, 1950/1, was £351·5 million and before the year started the government said this was to be a ceiling, above which expenditure was not to be allowed to rise. New developments and extensions of the service could only take place if equivalent savings were made elsewhere. At the end of the year expenditure turned out at £336·5 million, £15 million within the estimate, but the estimates for 1951/2 were up again – £355 million for England and Wales, nearly £400 million if Scotland were included. This figure of £400 million was one which the government had fixed as an absolute limit, and in order to keep within it in the face of costs which were continuing to rise, it was decided that certain charges to users of the service would have to be instituted.

Charges: drugs, dentures and spectacles

A prescription charge had been authorised by an amending Act of 1949, but had not been implemented, largely because of Aneurin Bevan's uncompromising opposition to any erosion of the principle of a free health service. As long as Sir Stafford Cripps was Chancellor of the Exchequer he was able to mediate between the Treasury view that charges were necessary both to offset some of the cost and to curb a tendency to prescribe medicines, spectacles and dentures too freely, and Bevan's opposition. However, in October 1950 Cripps resigned because of ill health, and Hugh Gaitskell, who had angered Bevan by pressing vigorously for charges, became Chancellor in his place. In January 1951 Bevan was persuaded to leave the Ministry of Health to become Minister of Labour. He was succeeded by H. A. Marquand, a former professor of industrial relations at University College, Cardiff, who had been first elected to Parliament in 1945 but had already held several government appointments. At this time the Ministry of Health was shorn of its responsibilities for housing and Marquand, unlike Bevan, was not a member of the Cabinet.

In the spring of 1951 the Act was further amended to allow charges for spectacles and dentures. In May, charges for spectacles and dentures, although not for drugs, were introduced, but on 22 April Aneurin Bevan and Harold Wilson had split the Labour Party by resigning from the Cabinet in protest against the health charges and increased spending on armaments. In October, Labour lost a general election, and the Conservatives, who had frequently alleged that health spending was out of control and was subject to widespread abuse, came to power. Early in the following year the new government introduced further legislation which, together with the 1949 amending Act, enabled them to impose charges for prescriptions, dental treatment, day nurseries, and a range of surgical appliances. To all these charges there were a number of exemptions, including nursing and expectant mothers and those under 21, as far as dental treatment – though not the supply of dentures – was concerned, and pensioners and persons receiving National Assistance as far as some or all of the charges were concerned.

Drugs, dentures and spectacles were emotive topics in these years. Not only did they account for an unexpectedly high proportion of the cost of the NHS, but there were doubts about whether these were the kind of things the NHS ought to be spending so much of its money on. Newspaper headlines fastened on wigs and dentures as examples of Socialist extravagance. Bevan made several appeals to the public not to abuse the service, but said, 'I shudder to think of the ceaseless cascade of medicine which is pouring down British throats at the present time. I wish I could believe that its efficacy was equal to the credulity with which it is being swallowed.'

Under the former National Health Insurance scheme some 23·3 million people were entitled not only to general medical services, but to free medicines, and in 1947 71·5 million prescriptions were dispensed under this arrangement. This figure was exceeded in the first six months of the NHS and in the first full year more than 200 million prescriptions were dispensed. Not only was the number of prescriptions rising, but so was the average cost, partly it seems because larger quantities were being prescribed, and partly because the more expensive proprietary preparations were being more frequently used. Knowing that any restriction on the doctor's right to prescribe whatever drug he thought best for his patient's treatment would be fiercely resisted, the ministry had to rely on persuasion in their attempts to ensure that proprietary drugs were not used where cheaper alternatives could be shown to have the same effect. However, the introduction of a one shilling charge for each prescription in 1952 checked the rise in the number of prescriptions – although to some extent doctors countered the charge by prescribing more items on each form – and also steadied the cost of the pharmaceutical service for the time being.

The NHS was launched at a time when many new and potent drugs were being brought into use. Many of the proprietary drugs which accounted for about half the total ingredient cost of all prescriptions fell under the headings of antibiotics and sulphonamide preparations which were making such a dramatic impact on bacterial infections of all kinds. Bevan pleaded with doctors not 'to evoke merely psychological response by prescribing too expensive drugs', but with more powerful therapeutic weapons at their disposal than they had had at any time in the past it seems probable that doctors were prescribing fewer rather than more placebos. The use of a powerful chemotherapeutic agent to deal with a minor infection might be criticised as taking a sledgehammer to crack a nut, but this is not the same as prescribing a bitter-tasting but innocuous liquid in order to convince the patient that he will get better.

If the sulphonamides and antibiotics heralded a therapeutic revolution, they were also the advance guard of a great army of new drugs of all kinds that were introduced from the 1950s onwards (see also Chapter 6). The introduction of phenothiazine and other tranquillising drugs, also in the early years of the NHS, helped to swell the number of prescriptions and the cost of dispensing them, as did new drugs to control such chronic conditions as diabetes mellitus, or high blood pressure. So it was that after the check given by the imposition of a prescription charge in 1952 – and in spite of the later substitution of a charge per item for a charge per form – both the number of prescriptions and the cost of the pharmaceutical service rose, until in the early 1970s more than 300 million prescriptions were being dispensed annually. The cost of the pharmaceutical service has been consistently around 10 per cent of the total cost of the NHS throughout the period under review, reaching 11 per cent in 1965 but falling again below 10 per cent in the early 1970s.

Under the National Health Insurance scheme before 1948 many but not all insured persons were entitled to dental benefit, although normally half or more of the cost of treatment had to be borne by the patient, with the result that many who were eligible for benefit did not avail themselves of it. Dental treatment for expectant and nursing mothers and for children under 5 was also provided, in varying degree, by most local welfare authorities, who did not charge for fillings or extractions, although a mother was usually expected to contribute towards the cost of any dentures supplied. Dental inspection and treatment for school children was provided by local education authorities as part of the school medical service.

Under the NHS most charges were abolished. At the inception of the service the only charges paid by patients were for dental treatment which in the view of the Dental Estimates Board (which had to approve all proposals for treatment involving dentures and other appliances) was more expensive than was strictly necessary, and for replacements necessitated by carelessness. The general dental service was not, and did not set out to be, a comprehensive service on a par with the general medical service. Patients did not register with dentists as they did with doctors, and each patient was free to go to any dentist of his choice for each course of treatment, as long as that dentist had entered into a contract with the executive council. Dentists were paid not by capitation fee, as were doctors, but by a scale of fees for services.

Estimates of the likely cost of the general dental service were based on experience of the National Health Insurance scheme, and although it was recognised that for only 6 to 7 per cent of those entitled to dental benefit to claim it each year was on the low side, the full extent of the demand that would be unleashed by offering free treatment and dentures to all who required them was by no means realised. The 1944 White Paper suggested it would be some years before the cost reached £10 million. In fact it was not even necessary to wait a full year. In the nine months from 5 July 1948 to 31 March 1949 the cost amounted to £39 million. In the first full year, 1949/50, it was £46·4 million, more than four-and-a-half times the original estimate. The ministry's first action to try to control the cost of the dental service was to cut the scales of fees on which dentists were paid. This action in 1949 helped to ensure that by 1950/1 the cost was down to £37·7 million and, further aided by the imposition of charges in 1951, it continued to fall for the next two years, after which it rose steadily in money terms, although remaining stable over the next two decades as a proportion of NHS expenditure. In 1949 the general dental service accounted for 10 per cent of all NHS spending, but from 1953 onwards for only about 5 per cent.

However, the cut in dentists' pay and the charges imposed on patients were not the only factors in the reduction of the cost of the dental service after 1951. Unlike most other aspects of the NHS the demand for dentures was self-limiting. By 1953, nearly 7 million people, or one in six of the population, were wearing a full set of dentures, nearly 6 million pairs of which had been issued under the NHS. Some people had more than one set of dentures, but none the less if we assume, as seems reasonable, that a high proportion of people who needed dentures had been fitted with them by 1953, 80 per cent had obtained their dentures since 1948, either as a first set or as replacements for unsatisfactory dentures fitted earlier.

Only about half of those insured under the National Health Insurance scheme were entitled to free or subsidised spectacles. Otherwise, apart from ophthalmic treatment provided for schoolchildren through the school medical service, those who required treatment or spectacles had to pay privately, or obtain them through the Poor Law or charitable sources. The 1944 White Paper suggested that the cost of the supplementary (i.e. non-hospital) ophthalmic service might rise towards £1 million several years after the inception of the NHS. This estimate was even wider of the mark than that for the dental service; in the first full year the supplementary ophthalmic service cost £20·1 million, of which the supply of spectacles accounted for more than 75 per cent. However, as with the dental service, the cost was falling even before the imposition of charges in 1951. Factors in this decrease included a reduction in the scale of fees for sight testing and a cheapening in the cost of spectacles. In the first nine months, people rushed to have their eyes tested, but there was a substantial fall in the number of tests carried out in 1951/2, and after 1948/9 a smaller proportion of tests resulted in a prescription for spectacles. In the early months it was 95 per cent. By 1953, about 19·5 million people had been supplied with 26·1 million pairs of spectacles.

The expansion of medicine

The unexpectedly high cost of a comprehensive health service and the fact that it appeared to be rising was a source not only of fierce political controversy between and within the parties, but also of some bewilderment to those who were reluctant to accept any of the more superficial diagnoses of Socialist profligacy and incompetence, or public abuse of the service on a truly massive scale. A more thoughtful attempt at explanation was offered in 1952 by Dr Ffrangcon Roberts in his book *The Cost of Health*. Roberts showed that Beveridge was wrong to assume that the demand for health care was finite and would fall as hitherto unmet needs were met. Medicine was expanding, new and more expensive methods of treatment were being developed, and the result of this expansion and development would not be the final conquest of disease, but only to leave doctors to contend with the more difficult problems of degenerative and chronic illness as more patients were enabled to reach old age. New and more sophisticated methods of diagnosis would change ideas on the nature of disease and great costs would be incurred as doctors felt obliged to use all the techniques at their disposal to establish beyond doubt what their patients were suffering from.

Medicine, Roberts argued, was subject to the law of diminishing returns. The easy problems were solved first, the cost of solving the more difficult problems would be infinitely higher. 'We are face to face with the paradox of unlimited progress towards an unattainable goal . . .'

The Guillebaud Report

In many of his interpretations and forecasts, Roberts has been shown to have been remarkably accurate. However, until the Guillebaud Committee reported in 1956 hardly anyone realised that to a very large extent the rise in health service costs since 1949 was an illusion, and Roberts was no exception. The Committee of Enquiry into the cost of the National Health Service was set up in May 1953 by the Conservative government which came to power in the autumn of 1951. Iain Macleod, a future Chancellor of the Exchequer, had by then taken over from Derek Walker-Smith as Minister of Health. The Committee were set up, amidst Opposition accusations that the Conservatives were seeking an excuse to mutilate the health service, with the following terms of reference:

To review the present and prospective cost of the National Health Service; to suggest means, whether by modifications in organisation or otherwise, of ensuring the most effective control and efficient use of such Exchequer funds as may be made available; to advise how, in view of the burden on the Exchequer, a rising charge upon it can be avoided while providing for the maintenance of an adequate Service; and to make recommendations.

The chairman was C. W. Guillebaud, a Cambridge economist, the members Dr J. W. Cook, a research chemist and Fellow of the Royal Society; Miss B. A. Godwin, general secretary of the Clerical and Administrative Workers' Union; Sir John Maude, a former permanent secretary of the Ministry of Health; and the industrialist Sir Geoffrey Vickers. Both members and terms of reference were well chosen to rebut the charge that the inquiry would be biased and devised to undermine the basis on which the NHS had been created. A further guarantee that if anything the Committee would lean over backwards to do justice to the ideals of the founders was the choice of Richard Titmuss and Brian Abel-Smith of the London School of Economics to carry out research for the committee. Titmuss was already well known as a

Socialist intellectual and Abel-Smith was later to become a principal adviser to Labour governments under Harold Wilson.

The Guillebaud Committee reported early in 1956 and the research carried out by Brian Abel-Smith, with Richard Titmuss as consultant, was published separately as an Occasional Paper on *The Cost of the National Health Service in England and Wales* by the National Institute of Economic and Social Research. The Committee relied heavily on Abel-Smith's researches, which showed that, once the fall in the value of money between 1949/50 and 1953/4 was allowed for, the rise in cost in 'real' terms over the four years was only £11 million, compared with the nominal rise of £59 million. Moreover, not only had the value of money fallen, but national income had increased quite considerably, and expressed as a proportion of gross national product the current net cost of the service had fallen from 3·75 per cent in 1949/50 to 3·25 per cent in 1953/4. It was also pointed out that the population had increased by nearly 2 per cent during the four years under review, and that the cost of the NHS per head of population was therefore, at constant prices, almost exactly the same in 1953/4 as in 1949/50.

This picture was, however, the net result of divergent trends in different parts of the service. The cost of the hospital service was rising, even at constant prices, and this was mainly accounted for by growth in the numbers of staff, particularly nurses and domestics. There was also some rise in the real cost of local authority health services, but a substantial fall in the cost of executive council services helped to offset both these increases. This saving reflected the apparent success of the dental and ophthalmic services in catching up with the backlog of demand for false teeth and spectacles. Concern was expressed that capital investment in the NHS had declined from 0·8 to 0·5 per cent of national fixed capital formation over the four years, in spite of the fact that 45 per cent of all hospitals had originally been erected before 1891 and many were seriously in need of replacement.

The Guillebaud Committee found that:

the Service's record of performance since the Appointed Day has been one of real achievement. The rising cost of the Service in real terms during the years 1948–54 were kept within narrow bounds; while many of the services provided were substantially expanded and improved during the period. Any charge that there has been widespread extravagance in the National Health Service, whether in respect of the spending of money or the use of manpower, is not borne out by our evidence.

In view of this finding, the Committee saw no need to recommend drastic change in organisation or financing. In any case, the NHS had only been in operation for seven years and it would be premature to propose any fundamental change. The service was only beginning to grapple with the deeper and wider problems that confronted it and some of the stresses and strains that were apparent were due, the Committee thought, to the difficulty experienced by many who had grown up under the old system, when called upon to operate a service organised on different lines. What was required was a period of stability so that authorities and their officers could begin to build for the future. In time to come, when further developments had taken place that could not then be foreseen, there might be a case for change, but the Guillebaud recommendations were designed to meet the situation, as they saw it, at that time.

Sir John Maude appended to the Report a reservation in which, whilst conceding that then was not the time for major change, he urged that none the less unification of the three parts of the NHS under local government should be clearly seen as the ultimate aim, even though this might only be possible after a reorganisation of local government itself which would have as one of its principal objects making local government administratively and financially able to accept responsibility for the NHS. Many years later, a Royal Commission on Local Government chaired by Sir John's near namesake, Lord Radcliffe-Maud, reported in favour of just such a reorganisation. Miss Godwin also signed the Guillebaud Report subject to a reservation, in her case recommending that the teaching hospitals should be taken under the wing of the RHBs, like their counterparts in Scotland. She also wanted abolished most of the charges to patients that had been imposed since 1948.

The Report offered a realistic assessment of what kind of health service the nation could expect:

> in the absence of an objective and attainable standard of adequacy the aim must be, as in the field of education, to provide the best service possible within the limits of the available resources . . . It is still sometimes assumed that the Health Service can and should be self-limiting, in the sense that its own contribution to national health will limit the demands upon it to a volume which can be fully met. This, at least for the present, is an illusion. It is equally illusory to imagine that everything which is desirable for the improvement of the Health Service can be achieved at once.

It was an impressive report and the minister's tribute to the members of the Committee for the 'very thorough and efficient way' they had tackled their task was well deserved. Most of the criticisms came from those who were disappointed that particular changes had not been recommended or that the health service had been given a clean sheet as far as financial extravagance was concerned. However, apart from the broad conclusion that structural change was not called for at that time, there were a number of recommendations on which action was subsequently taken and many of the topics which were examined with some care by the Guillebaud Committee emerged as prominent items on the agenda for discussion and controversy over the next two decades.

The Committee were by no means complacent about the disadvantages inherent in the tripartite structure of the service. There were difficulties in co-ordinating the three parts, there was a danger of duplication and overlap, but apart from the question of the timeliness of any reorganisation the Committee did not believe that closer integration would necessarily be achieved by unifying the service in each part of the country under one administrative body. 'Any administrative system', they wisely remarked, 'has inherent in it the problem of securing a proper co-ordination of its various parts, and the transfer of statutory responsibility to a single authority will not in itself do much to solve the problem.' But in one particular case there was perhaps more urgency. The maternity services were 'in a state of some confusion, which must impair their usefulness, and which should not be allowed to continue'. A separate body should be set up to review the maternity service to find out precisely what was required and how it might best be provided within the framework of the NHS. In due course the Cranbrook Committee were appointed to review the maternity services – although in their Report they did not agree that these services were 'in a state of some confusion'.

In the interests of better financial management at local level the Guillebaud Committee recommended the introduction in the hospital service of a system of departmental costing which would allow heads of departments to see the costs they were incurring in a way which was not possible under the traditional subjective accounting system. They also urged that attention be given to the recruitment and training of hospital administrators and to the establishment of a career structure for them. As a result of this recommendation Sir Noel Hall was asked to prepare a report on the grading structure of administrative and clerical staff in the hospital service. His report is discussed in Chapter 7.

The level of services provided for the aged were a matter for concern, but their inadequacy reflected a lack of resources rather than problems of organisation. The needs of the aged must be given due priority, but deficiencies would not be remedied overnight. The question of private beds in NHS hospitals was considered, but no change was thought to be necessary. There were problems with the ambulance service, but no advantage was seen in transferring ambulances from the local authorities to the hospitals. The Committee were offered a number of criticisms of the Whitley Councils which determined the pay and conditions of service of staff in the NHS, but they were hopeful that as experience was gained and the service settled down, the Whitley system would work more smoothly than in the past. On several topics the Committee or their researchers found that the information they needed simply was not available, so one of the final recommendations was that the Health Departments (the Ministry of Health for England and Wales and the Scottish Home and Health Department) should set up a Research and Statistics Department which would consider what information was lacking as to the working of the NHS, and how it might best be produced.

3
A Special Relationship – the Professions and the NHS

*'Some people say that we must not kick a man when he is down.
Why not? He's still breathing isn't he?'* Dr Roland Cockshut,
during the 1946–8 controversy between Aneurin Bevan and
the doctors

'You want the doctors, we *have* the doctors', Dr Guy Dain, chairman
of the Council of the British Medical Association, told Bevan, and while
subsequent events suggested that the hold which Dr Dain and his
colleagues had on the membership at large was rather less firm than they
might have wished, it remained indisputably true that the NHS could
not function without doctors. To some extent it could not function
without other grades of staff either, but length of training and the
legislation governing the practice of medicine meant that it would have
been much more difficult to find substitutes for doctors than for almost
any other grade of staff. So the relationship between the health service
and the medical profession has always been a particularly crucial one.
However, in this chapter we shall examine not only that relationship,
but also the dealings of the health service with other professions and
groups of staff. The administrators, and members of the medical and
nursing professions occupying mainly administrative posts, will alone
be left for consideration in Chapter 7.

The NHS is and has been since its inception labour-intensive and one
of the world's largest employers. In 1949 the NHS employed, in England
and Wales, just over half a million people, by 1973 the figure was more
than 0·9 million, or about one in thirty of the population of working age.
Over the period the proportion of health service spending accounted for
by salaries and wages rose from just under 60 to around 70 per cent.

Both hospital doctors and hospital nurses more than doubled, in terms of whole-time equivalents, between 1949 and 1973, as did hospital administrative and clerical staff. Hospital midwives nearly doubled, while professional and technical staff (the group which includes the paramedical professions, laboratory and other technicians etc.) increased by almost three times. Outside the hospitals, the numbers of general medical practitioners showed little variation between 1949 and 1973, while general dental practitioners increased by about 20 per cent. Local authority nurses rather less than doubled, while health visitors increased by about 75 per cent.

Some of the changes within these various categories were also significant. In 1949, 30 per cent of hospital doctors were on the consultant grade; by 1973 the proportion was 36 per cent. Among hospital nurses, the proportion of nursing auxiliaries and nursing assistants, the grades having no or only minimal training, rose from 20 to nearly 30 per cent. Furthermore, the increases were not distributed evenly over the period; for several groups of staff the trend accelerated in the late 1960s and early 1970s. Nursing staff, for example, were increasing by about 3·7 per cent per annum up to 1969, but between 1969 and 1973 the average rate was 4·5 per cent per annum. Hospital doctors increased on average by about 3·7 per cent per annum until 1969, but between 1969 and 1973 the rate was 4·7 per cent. On the other hand, the most rapid increase in hospital ancillary staff took place in the first ten years of the NHS and by 1969–73 the annual rate of increase had slowed to just over one per cent, to some extent offsetting the more rapid rates of growth of other groups of staff.

DOCTORS AND DENTISTS

Aneurin Bevan set out his view of the relations between doctors and the NHS in a speech to the Royal Medico-Psychological Association a few weeks after he became Minister of Health. 'I conceive it', he said, 'the function of the Ministry of Health to provide the medical profession with the best and most modern apparatus of medicine and to enable them freely to use it, in accordance with their training, for the benefit of the people of the country. Every doctor must be free to use that apparatus without interference from secular organisations.' This was a view entirely acceptable to the doctors and it became an object of professional policy to try to ensure that the NHS provided doctors with the means to apply the most advanced techniques of modern medicine, without stint or any attempt at control, whilst the doctors themselves maintained the stance of independent professional men and women, making use of the NHS organisation but not part of it. The general practitioners had indeed the legal status of independent contractors, but few consultants allowed the fact that they were now paid a salary for services they had previously given, as far as the voluntary hospitals were concerned, gratis, to affect their attitude that the hospital was their workshop and that it was the business of the hospital authorities to meet their requirements, and not vice versa. The fact that doctors were well represented among members of the new hospital authorities assisted in the maintenance of this stance, as did the fact that outside the teaching groups senior medical staff were employed by the regional hospital boards rather than by the hospital management committees in whose hospitals they worked.

The Spens Committees

Two years before the National Health Service Act came into effect the government set up three Committees, each under the chairmanship of Sir Will Spens, to report on what ought to be the range of incomes of general medical practitioners, general dental practitioners, and consultants and specialists, in the new service. When the Reports appeared, all three Committees expressed their recommendations in 1939 money values, leaving 'to others the problem of the necessary adjustments to present-day values of money', but with the clear implication that doctors and dentists should be protected against the effects of inflation.

The Committee on general medical practitioners recommended that between 40 and 50 years of age about 50 per cent of doctors should receive net incomes of £1,300 a year (1939 values) or over. Three-quarters of all general practitioners would earn over £1,000 and one-quarter over £1,600. A small number should be able to earn at least £2,500. All these figures referred to gross income, less practice expenses. The British Medical Association estimated that the translation of these figures into postwar money values should be on the basis of a betterment figure of 100 per cent. The ministry offered 60 per cent. In 1951 the still unresolved dispute was referred to a High Court judge for arbitration, and Mr Justice Danckwerts found in favour of the doctors. His award was accepted by the Conservative government in the following year.

It was a complicated matter to translate an award expressed in terms of average earnings into actual payments when it had been agreed that doctors should be paid capitation fees, plus certain additional fees for maternity work, part-time work for the local authority and in hospitals, as well as from private practice, rather than a salary. This is how it was done: the agreed average net income was multiplied by the number of doctors, and an agreed amount for practice expenses was added to this total pool; deductions were then made for general practitioners' estimated earnings from other sources, and the money that was left was distributed in the form of capitation fees and supplementary allowances of various kinds.

The three Spens Committees worked independently, so the fact that the Committee on consultants and specialists recommended a salary of at least £2,500 (1939 values) for a full-time consultant at about 40, compared with the £1,300 envisaged for a general practitioner of the same age, could not be taken as implying any considered conclusion on the appropriate differential between the two branches of the profession. It none the less reflected the fact that before the war there had been a differential, although it had been narrowing. A problem that did concern this Committee was the wide spread of earnings among consultants themselves, too wide to embody in an acceptable salary scale. The solution to this problem was the system of distinction awards to recognise special contributions to medicine, exceptional ability, or outstanding professional work. It was suggested there should be three grades of award; the top grade would be worth £2,500 a year (1939 values), thus doubling the recipient's salary. Once given an award, a consultant would keep it until he retired, and it would be taken into account in calculating his pension. The awards would be administered by a predominantly professional committee – in the event all the members were doctors, and the first chairman was Lord Moran, president of the Royal College of Physicians, who was succeeded in 1962 by Lord Brain. The awards were adjusted from time to time to take account of inflation and consultant pay generally. The awards, and the deliberations which led up to them, were confidential, but they were based on extensive consultations with members of the various specialties. The system was from time to time criticised for leaving the power to spend large sums of public money in the hands of a professional committee, and for appearing to favour certain specialties more than others. It was, however, at least arguable that certain specialties attracted more able doctors than others, and that apparent discrimination against, for instance, geriatrics merely reflected the distribution of ability within the profession.

The Committee on consultants and specialists also looked at specialists in training, and made recommendations for the pay of grades that came to be generally known as senior house officer, registrar, and senior registrar. These grades, the Committee thought, had been substantially underpaid in the past. In the public service, the Committee urged, 'specialists who do not possess private means should not be called upon to pass through a stage of comparative penury and hardship. Nor should they be tempted to spend too much time in supplementing their income from other sources, such as coaching, when they could be more suitably occupied in their professional studies.' They therefore recommended the payment to the trainee specialist of a salary 'which is not merely in the nature of a training grant but which reflects both the growth in his skill and the increasing responsibility of his work'.

The third Spens Committee, on general dental practitioners, had before them the report of the Committee on general medical practitioners, and they suggested it would be appropriate if dentists' fees were calculated on a basis which would allow them to earn a little less than the doctors. The calculations should further assume that 33 hours a week by the chairside for 46 weeks in the year represented for the dentist full but not excessive employment.

The Pilkington Report

In spite of the Danckwerts award, and in spite of the fact that it somewhat reduced the gap between the incomes of consultants and general practitioners which had been envisaged by Spens, there was much unrest on questions of pay within the medical profession in the 1950s and this unrest culminated in the appointment of a Royal Commission on Doctors' and Dentists' Remuneration (the Pilkington Commission), which reported in 1960. Apart from recommending a general increase of about 21 per cent, and certain modifications in the system for calculating the general practitioners' 'pool', the Pilkington Commission recommended the setting up of a small Standing Review Body, independent of the ministry and the NHS, to keep doctors' and dentists' pay under review and to make recommendations from time to time. The pay and conditions of other groups of NHS staff were negotiated on a series of national Whitley Councils, but the Whitley Council for doctors and dentists had never functioned as a negotiating body, having been bypassed when the professional organisations insisted on negotiating directly with the ministry. This had led to a series of heated disputes and threats of extreme action by the professional organisations, and the Pilkington recommendation of an independent review body was an attempt to lower the temperature and to provide a system for determining doctors' and dentists' pay that would command the confidence of both sides.

The Standing Review Body was set up in 1962, under the chairmanship of Lord Kindersley, a banker, and functioned, with various changes of membership, throughout the period under review. In the first instance the members included an eminent lawyer, an actuary, two non-medical professors, and two financiers; as the Review Body was to be entirely independent, no doctors were included. The Review Body was to report not to the Minister of Health, but to the Prime Minister. The Review Body's first report was produced, following submissions from the professions, in 1963, and subsequent reports were produced at intervals of two to three years. The setting up of the Review Body by no means marked the end of disputes over doctors' and dentists' pay – indeed the first report sparked off a major row with the general practitioners – but it is now necessary to retrace our steps to discuss aspects other than pay.

Problems of general practice

In the discussions leading up to the establishment of the NHS, general practitioners were on the whole more militant than the consultants, and throughout the 1950s and early 1960s there was more discontent among general practitioners than among the consultant body. In the late 1960s and early 1970s the position was reversed. However, the 1950s were also characterised by concern about the career problems of hospital registrars and senior registrars and the first sounds of serious discontent among junior doctors generally, sounds that were to mount to a crescendo in the late 1960s.

The general practitioners were no longer willing to accept the traditional differential between a general practitioner's income and that of a consultant, and they were resentful when the Pilkington Commission recommended that the ratio should be 3:2 in favour of the consultant. In 1952 the founding of the College (later Royal College) of General Practitioners represented an attempt to create a body of the same standing as the older Royal Colleges of Physicians, Surgeons, and Obstetricians and Gynaecologists. The argument was put to the Pilkington Commission that consultants and general practitioners were not senior and junior branches of the profession, but equal in terms of status and responsibility. When this view was put to Lord Moran, president of the Physicians, he commented: 'Could anything be more absurd? . . . How can you say that the people who get to the top of the ladder are the same as the people who fall off it?' This remark did not endear him to the general practitioners, who pressed their claims for recognition to such effect that in 1968 the Todd Commission on Medical Education tied themselves in semantic knots by recognising general practice as a specialty in its own right, and the general practitioner as a 'specialist'.

At the outset of the NHS there was concern at the variability of standards in general practice, and several surveys in the early years showed that some doctors were practising from premises lacking even basic amenities, and with quite inadequate equipment. At that time, doctors were paid on a basis which assumed they would provide their own premises and equipment, and so those who spent little in this way were adding to their own disposable income at the expense of their patients. Marked improvements in the accommodation and equipment used by many general practitioners did not come about until after 1966, when a system was instituted which reimbursed doctors for practice expenses, and an increasing number of doctors started to work from health centres and group practice premises.

In spite of the duty laid on local authorities under the National Health Service Act to provide health centres, the unwillingness of doctors to work in them and financial stringency in local government combined to ensure that few were built in the early years. However, the 1966 agreement between the government and the profession on a 'Charter for the Family Doctor Service' included the offer of special payments to doctors who combined into groups using common premises and employing ancillary staff, and at the same time the increasing cost of land and building was making it more difficult for doctors to provide their own premises. By the end of 1969 there were more health centres under construction than had been built in the whole of the previous twenty-one years.

Junior hospital doctors
The registrar and senior registrar problem reached crisis proportions in the very early years of the NHS. These grades were intended as training grades, and by the time a doctor had spent two years as a registrar and three as a senior registrar it was assumed he would normally secure an appointment as a consultant. By 1950 there were 2,800 registrars and senior registrars, and only twice that number of consultant posts in the whole NHS. Time-expired senior registrars were therefore unable to secure consultant posts, especially as they were also in competition with those of the 2,000 or so doctors in the senior hospital medical officer grade who were anxious to become consultants. The SHMO grade was not a training grade, but a permanent grade of sub-consultant status, devised as a means of absorbing those doctors already employed in 1948 but not considered of consultant calibre.

When the Ministry of Health tried to force hospital authorities to terminate the employment of time-expired senior registrars and registrars who failed to secure posts in the next higher grade, an indignant reaction from the profession forced them to retract, and to allow time-expired senior registrars to be retained on a year-to-year basis while they sought consultant appointments. One possible solution would have been to increase the number of consultant posts, but the ministry were not anxious to adopt any solution which would increase NHS costs, and there were many consultants who would have opposed any great expansion in consultant numbers, particularly as this would have meant more intense competition for the limited amount of private practice.

In 1955 a Committee were set up under the chairmanship of Sir Henry Willink, the former Minister of Health, to consider how many doctors the country needed and what the appropriate intake of medical students would therefore be. The Willink Committee, which reported in 1957, concluded that too many doctors were being trained, and that the number of medical school places should be reduced by 10 per cent. Already, in fact, the numbers of medical students had started to decline, so the government's acceptance of the Willink recommendation did not involve any further drastic action. However, the Willink Committee had been working from faulty data. Many more young doctors were emigrating than they had allowed for, and they did not take into account the implications for medical staffing of the rapid developments in medical technology of which Dr Ffrangcon Roberts had written so eloquently (see Chapter 2). By 1961 the ministry had decided it was necessary to increase the number of medical students by 10 per cent, but this was too late to prevent British hospitals from experiencing a severe shortage of junior medical staff throughout the 1960s. This shortage was only ameliorated by the employment of large numbers of doctors from India, Pakistan and other Commonwealth countries, a remedy which brought its own problems, particularly when the newcomers had only a meagre command of the English language.

Wider grounds for discontent among junior doctors as a whole – and not merely the registrar and senior registrar grades – were set out in a book, *Angry Young Doctor*, published in 1957 by Louis Goldman, a 35-year-old South African doctor who drew on his experience of living and working in seven British hospitals between 1951 and 1956. He described the house officer as

> a doctor who is compelled to live and work in a hospital for at least one year, generally under conditions which can only be described as primitive; whose hours of duty are fixed without possibility of alteration at approximately one hundred per week; who performs responsible work but has no status; who does what he is told but has no means of redress; and who, having completed his term of service, is discharged and thereafter left to fend for himself.

'This is not merely forced labour', he wrote, 'this is exploitation.' His theme was to be taken up with increasing force over the next decade, and discontent among junior doctors led to the formation of a Junior Hospital Doctors Association and to more forceful representations on behalf of junior doctors by the BMA. By the time the NHS was reorganised junior doctors' pay and conditions had improved considerably.

Medical education

The medical schools as such had not been nationalised along with the associated teaching hospitals in 1948. They remained the responsibility of the University Grants Committee; none the less the relationship between the medical schools, medical education and the NHS was necessarily an interdependent one. Medical staffing structures had implications for medical education, especially at postgraduate level, and it was a matter of continuing controversy what proportion of teaching hospital costs could reasonably be attributed to their teaching function. However, the first comprehensive review of medical education since the inception of the NHS did not take place until 1965–8, when the Royal Commission on Medical Education deliberated under the chairmanship of Lord Todd.

The Todd Report recommended that the annual intake to medical schools should be more than doubled by 1990, and that while existing medical schools should be expanded, new schools should be created at Southampton, Leicester, Nottingham, Swansea, and possibly later at Stoke-on-Trent, Hull, Norwich and Coventry. Radical recommendations on both undergraduate and postgraduate medical education were accompanied by proposals for changes in the medical staffing structure which included the establishment in the hospital service of two grades of fully responsible doctor, the specialist and the consultant, in place of the single grade of consultant which at that time was the only grade not working, at least nominally, under the supervision of a consultant. It was proposed that postgraduate training would be divided into two phases: three years of general professional training, much of which would be common to all or a number of specialties; followed by a further period, normally of two years, of supervised practice as a junior specialist. The three years' general professional training would be preceded by an intern year in which the young doctor would gain his first taste of clinical responsibility.

By the time the NHS was reorganised, changes had been made in undergraduate curricula as a result of the Todd recommendations, but changes in postgraduate training were taking longer to effect. The proposal to establish two grades of fully responsible doctor had not proved acceptable to the profession; by 1974, however, the government had agreed to a steady but significant expansion of consultant numbers. The problem which remained with no sign of solution was that of the distribution of consultants between specialties. In many parts of the country, particularly those which are not particularly attractive to professional people, such as the North West and Merseyside, consultant appointments in geriatrics and psychiatry remained unfilled for long periods, while there was intense competition for such appointments in more popular specialties and more popular parts of the country. Similarly, a system of incentive payments to persuade general practitioners to live and work in under-doctored areas had achieved but limited success, and wide variations in average list size remained.

NURSES AND MIDWIVES

The nursing profession were by no means in the same position to hold out for terms in negotiation with the government as were the doctors in the years leading up to 1948. On the other hand, relations between the government and the profession were good and nurses could see that they stood to gain from the establishment of a national service in place of a multiplicity of voluntary hospitals and local authorities, varying widely in their resources and in the salaries they were able or willing to pay. During the Second World War the Ministry of Health laid down minimum salaries or training allowances for trained and student nurses and gave subsidies to the voluntary hospitals to enable them to pay these rates. In 1941 the Rushcliffe Committee were set up to negotiate nurses' pay in England and Wales, and the Guthrie Committee in Scotland. With the establishment of the NHS, both these Committees were replaced by the Nurses and Midwives Whitley Council, consisting of a management side and a staff side, and charged with negotiating salaries and conditions of service for nurses working both for hospital authorities and for local health authorities. At the same time, other Whitley Councils were set up for ancillary staffs, administrative and clerical staffs, and for the various groupings of paramedical and technical staff.

The Wood Report
Immediately before the NHS the recruitment and training of nurses had been reviewed by the Wood Committee, whose Report was published in 1947. The Committee called for more careful selection of would-be nurses, as well as changes in the structure of training and in nurses' conditions, in order to try to reduce the figure of 54 per cent of student nurses who failed to complete their training. The training for the Register, the Committee recommended, should be reduced from three years to two by relieving student nurses of domestic work and repetitive duties which contributed little to their training but which were dictated solely by the staffing needs of the hospitals. Student nurses should be students in more than name, and not merely junior employees subject to an outmoded system of discipline. They should work a five-day week of 40 hours, instead of the 48 which were then customary, and they should have six weeks' holiday a year. After completing her two-year training and passing her examinations the nurse would be given the pay and status of a State Registered Nurse, but would have

to work a further year under supervision before being licensed to practise independently.

The Wood Report recommended that the Roll of Assistant Nurses, which had only been set up under the Nurses Act of 1943, should be closed, and the duties undertaken by assistant nurses should be allocated partly to trained staff and partly to nursing orderlies, a grade with no formal training. To implement the proposed reforms, the number of trained nurses in employment should be increased from 88,000 to 112,000. The Committee thought this would be possible if wastage during training were reduced, if all restrictions on the employment of married nurses then in force were lifted, and if the use of male nurses were extended.

This brave new world did not come to pass. Powerful elements in the profession were opposed to the separation of training schools from the hospitals which the Wood Committee had envisaged. Hospital authorities could not see their way to granting full student status and thus doing without the contribution made by student nurses to the routine work of the hospitals. The 1949 Nurses Act created an area nurse training committee in each hospital region, but these committees were vested with few of the powers which the Wood Committee had envisaged for the proposed regional nurse training boards. The Roll of Assistant Nurses was not abolished, although in 1950 the training was reduced from two years to one year, followed by a further year of work under supervision, and eventually the word 'assistant' was dropped from the title of the State Enrolled Nurse. The length of training for the Register remained at three years, although the 1949 Act empowered the General Nursing Council to approve experimental schemes of training.

Nurses' pay and conditions and the training given to student nurses and pupil nurses (i.e. those training for the Registers and the Roll respectively) improved only gradually. A good deal of information on the practical training received by student nurses was yielded by a study, *The Work of Nurses in Hospital Wards*, published by the Nuffield Provincial Hospitals Trust in 1953. This study, based on minute-by-minute observation, found that ward sisters spent very little time teaching student nurses, unless it was assumed that all the time a ward sister was working within sight of a student nurse she was in fact teaching by example. This finding was hotly contested, but subsequent studies tended to confirm that there was room for improvement in both the standard and the amount of practical training that student nurses received. The situation only improved with the introduction in the early 1960s of clinical instructors, trained nurses working in the wards with a specific responsibility for teaching student nurses and, unlike the ward sisters and staff nurses, no administrative load to carry.

The Platt Report

Further radical proposals for changes in nurse training came from a Committee set up in 1961 by the Royal College of Nursing under the chairmanship of Sir Harry Platt. The Platt Report, entitled *A Reform of Nursing Education*, was widely regarded outside nursing circles as pie in the sky, an extreme statement of professional aspirations that took little account of practical or economic realities. In some respects, however, it was less extreme than the Wood Report seventeen years previously. Its thinking retained the separate registers for general, mental and sick children's nurses, which the Wood Committee had wanted to merge, although it suggested it might be possible to design a common training for the nursing of the mentally ill and the mentally handicapped. There were curious touches of conservatism, such as the insistence that student nurses, both men and women, should normally be required to be resident during the first two years of their course. The Platt Committee were close to Wood in their recommendation that student nurses should enjoy full student status for the first two years of their training, and should take the final examination at the end of those two years. The third year should be spent in supervised experience, six months in general medical or surgical nursing, and six months in a specialty of the student's choice. The Roll of Nurses would remain, but a new grade, the ward assistant, would be prepared by means of an in-service training to provide a service ancillary to nursing and to replace the nursing auxiliaries (in general hospitals) and nursing assistants (in mental hospitals) who were regarded professionally with suspicion because of the word 'nursing' in their title and the dilution of the profession which this was held to represent.

National Board for Prices and Incomes

In 1968 the system of nursing education was also criticised by the National Board for Prices and Incomes, which had been set up two years previously by the Labour government as part of their attempt to control inflation. References to the Board were generally designed to procure an examination of whether particular wage increases, or proposed wage increases, were justified and in accordance with government economic policy. The pay of nurses and midwives in the NHS was referred to the Board in July 1967 at the expiration of a two-year salary settlement. A major claim for a general increase, as well as a number of specific claims for improvements in hours and conditions of work, had been made by the staff organisations. At the same time, the Board were asked to report on the proposed salary scales for the new grade of chief nursing officer, recommended by the Salmon Committee (see Chapter 7).

For most nursing grades, the Board recommended increases averaging

9 per cent, but found no evidence of a general shortage of nurses. There were shortages in particular grades and particular hospitals; there was mismanagement of resources and 'a diffusion of authority and a fragmented system of management which make it difficult to increase efficiency in the hospital'. The Board's recommendations for the management of the nursing service will be discussed in Chapter 7, but the Board recommended that the age of entry to training should be lowered from 18 to 17 years in England and Wales ($17\frac{1}{2}$ to 17 in Scotland). In the longer term, larger group nurse training schools should be set up, independent of the management of particular hospitals – this would largely resolve the problem of the supposed shortage of nurse tutors, which on examination turned out to be mainly one of maldistribution, and the uneconomic use of tutors in small schools.

There was little in the Report which was original; at times it read like a digest of the 'progressive' thought of the previous twenty years – straight shift systems of working, the abolition of unnecessary restrictions in nurses' homes, increased use of part-time staff, the setting up of a National Nursing Management Council to supervise the introduction of new working methods – but the Board's views carried considerable authority with the government and many of the recommendations were either accepted by the Department of Health or, where appropriate, commended to hospital authorities. The National Nursing Management Council was not set up, probably because more sweeping changes in the NHS as a whole then appeared to be imminent, and the age of commencement of training was, of course, a matter for the General Nursing Councils rather than the ministry.

The Briggs Report

A more balanced view of wastage during training was taken by the Briggs Committee on Nursing, which reported in 1972. The Committee observed that although one student nurse in three failed to complete her training, and this rate was higher than for trainee teachers and for students in higher education, it represented a lower rate of turnover than usually found among young women at work. There was, however, scope for improvement, through better working conditions, and above all by raising the quality and quantity of training. This the Briggs Committee proposed to do by establishing a basic course designed to produce at the end of eighteen months a safe and confident practical nurse, able to work as a basic member of the nursing team in any field of nursing. Following basic training, those nurses who wished and had the ability to do so would proceed to a further eighteen months' training for Registration, possibly preparing at the same time for a Higher Certificate which would be recognised as an advanced qualification in a particular field of nursing. If taken after Registration, the Higher Certificate course would last six months. The aim was a flexible structure of training, constructed on modular principles, which would enable nursing to recruit from a wide spectrum of ability and to offer each recruit a training suitable for her capacities and her career goals. The training would be based on Colleges of Nursing and Midwifery, with their own governing bodies, although a proportion of nurses would receive their professional education in universities and colleges where degrees in nursing had already been established or might be established in the future.

Halsbury award

The Briggs recommendations had not been implemented by the time the NHS was reorganised, but the profession were pressing vigorously for their acceptance by the Department of Health, and the then Secretary of State, Barbara Castle, was sympathetic. She was also receptive to the vigorously expressed feeling that nurses had fallen behind in the pay race and during 1974 she commissioned Lord Halsbury, who was then chairman of the Standing Review Body on doctors' and dentists' pay, to conduct a special investigation and report to her on nurses' pay.

Lord Halsbury worked quickly and within months he had recommended substantial increases, the detailed application of which then had to be worked out through the Whitley machinery. Nurses were on the whole very pleased with the Halsbury award, but there were particular groups that did less well than they had hoped, and some anomalies which may have reflected the speed with which Lord Halsbury worked, as well as the extreme complexity of the grading structure evolved over the years.

PROFESSIONS SUPPLEMENTARY TO MEDICINE

Towards the end of 1974 Lord Halsbury was also asked to look at the pay and conditions of service of a number of paramedical professions which, like the nurses, felt they had fallen behind. These were professions that had come into existence to carry out particular forms of treatment or investigations on behalf of doctors, who continued to take overall responsibility for the patient. A few months after the inception of the NHS a series of eight Committees were set up to consider the supply and demand, training and qualifications, of almoners, chiropodists, dietitians, medical laboratory technicians, occupational therapists, physiotherapists (including remedial gymnasts, who none the less had a separate training and their own professional organisation); radiographers; and speech therapists. Dr (later Sir) Zachary Cope was chairman of all eight Committees and in 1951 there were published not only eight separate Reports, one for each of the professions considered, but also a general Report on 'matters common to all types of medical auxiliary service'. The general Report proposed there should be a statutory register of persons qualified for employment as medical auxiliaries in the NHS, and that a statutory body should be set up under the aegis of the Privy Council to perform this and other functions.

This proposal eventually bore fruit in the Professions Supplementary to Medicine Act 1960, and in the setting up of the Council for Professions Supplementary to Medicine, with seven Boards, each serving a particular profession. By this time it was no longer considered appropriate to class almoners as medical auxiliaries, or, in the new terminology, a profession supplementary to medicine, and they were not included. In due course almoners developed closer links with other types of social worker, and their future was discussed in the 1968 Report of the Seebohm Committee on Local Authority and Allied Personal Social Services.

Throughout the 1960s and early 1970s questions were being asked about the future of the professions supplementary to medicine. History and the emergence of separate professional organisations had conspired to give each of them a distinct sense of professional identity, yet the work of, for example, occupational therapists, physiotherapists and remedial gymnasts overlapped heavily, and there seemed to be powerful arguments that they should experience at least part of their training in common. The Oddie Committee, which reported in 1970, had been set up by the Council for Professions Supplementary to Medicine to consider the question of closer integration between these three professions, and they admitted that if it had been possible to start with a clean slate logic would have suggested the creation of one profession, not three. They noted too that there had over the years been 'expressions of goodwill, and a general wish for a closer relationship, but few, if any, concrete proposals for action', but they did not themselves put forward any firm solutions, only suggestions for discussion. They did, however, conclude that a common basic course of training for the three professions would be feasible.

This conclusion was supported by the Tunbridge Committee on the Remedial Professions, set up by the Department of Health, when they presented a brief statement in lieu of a formal report in 1972. One reason for this informal report was that the Committee had strayed outside their terms of reference to identify four principal areas of difficulty affecting the remedial professions. These were: (1) remuneration; (2) career structure; (3) professional role; and (4) research. Pay was, the Committee declared, low in comparison with other professions of equivalent responsibility and educational background, and no longer sufficient to attract and retain good recruits of both sexes. The professional role of the remedial professions was unclear, and while the treatment they administered was prescribed by doctors many therapists felt that they were at times required to give treatment that was inadequate or ineffective without being able to discuss the matter with the prescribing doctor. There was a serious lack of research into the effectiveness of various forms of remedial and rehabilitative treatment.

As the Tunbridge Committee had failed to produce any firm proposals for the future, the Secretary of State, Sir Keith Joseph, invited the professional bodies to set up a working party with officers of the Department of Health to see if they could move things forward. The working party were convened in March 1973 and reported in October that the three professions were at a point of crisis that could only be resolved by the firm prospect of positive action. The Society of Remedial Gymnasts and the Chartered Society of Physiotherapists should go ahead with their proposed merger, and this should be regarded as the first step towards unifying the three professions, with a common basic training. The working party also called for a new career and salary structure and for a new, more independent relationship with the medical profession. Action on these recommendations had necessarily to wait until after NHS reorganisation.

SCIENTIFIC AND TECHNICAL GROUPS

In addition to these three remedial professions, the professions supplementary to medicine also include such groups as the radiographers and medical laboratory technicians who are more conveniently discussed along with the other scientific and technical grades whose futures were considered in the 1968 Zuckerman Report on Hospital Scientific and Technical Services. This report proposed a unified career and grading structure for a large number of professional and sub-professional groups, many of which had emerged in response to the development of new medical technologies. Altogether the Zuckerman Committee identified about thirty groups of staff, numbering about 27,000, as falling within their terms of reference. The basic proposal was that a Hospital Scientific Service should be set up to embrace the four main branches of pathology and the biological sciences; nuclear medicine and medical physics; biomedical engineering; and applied physiology. The service would include medically and non-medically qualified staff.

The implication of the Zuckerman proposals for such well-established groups as the radiographers, medical laboratory technicians and orthoptists was that enhanced career prospects and membership of a unified scientific service might have to be paid for with some loss of professional autonomy. For this and other reasons progress on the implementation of the Zuckerman recommendations was slow, although the Department of Health's guidance to the reorganised health authorities set up in 1973 suggested that in each region there should be a regional scientific committee to advise on the planning and organisation of all scientific services, and that similar committees should be set up at area level.

4

The Rise of the District General Hospital

. . . the Piraeus, which was as orderly, as regular and as dull as 'town-planned' towns generally are, for Hippodamos of Miletus the planner was a philosopher, and there is nothing worse than the architect-townplanner with philosophical theories. J. S. Stobart, *The Glory That Was Greece*

Of the 2,800 hospitals, with rather more than 500,000 beds, which were vested in the minister on 5 July 1948, 45 per cent were originally built before 1891 and 21 per cent before 1861. As we saw in Chapter 1, many of them, especially among the former voluntary hospitals, were small, and about one in three of the former voluntary hospitals specialised in a particular branch of medicine or surgery. Half the former local authority beds were in the 300 or so, often very large, hospitals for the mentally ill or handicapped and many of the other ex-municipal hospitals were former Poor Law institutions or infirmaries that still bore all too clearly the marks of their origin.

Nineteenth-century conditions and problems thus largely dictated the stock of buildings in which the NHS set out to tackle the problems of the mid-twentieth century. The discovery of anaesthesia had expanded the scope of surgery and helped to create a feeling that each locality should have quick and easy access to at least a small hospital where general practitioners could operate on or simply care for their patients in better conditions than were often obtainable in the patients' homes. The cottage hospital movement gathered momentum from the 1860s onwards, but by 1948 advances in surgery and anaesthesia were rapidly putting all but the simplest surgical procedures outside the scope of a general practitioner working in a cottage hospital.

Similarly, many of the special hospitals were founded by doctors – sometimes reacting against the refusal of the general hospitals to recognise the line of work in which they were engaged as a speciality meriting its own consultant appointment – or by philanthropists with an interest in a specific type of affliction. The Chandler sisters, instrumental in founding the National Hospital for Nervous Diseases, were perhaps the best known example of the latter situation. Many of the special hospitals made outstanding contributions to medical progress, but by 1948 there were many who were prepared to argue that further advances within a specialty might best be achieved by bringing it within the purview of a general hospital and into closer association with other branches of medicine or surgery.

Furthermore, nineteenth-century transport patterns made it essential that a general hospital receiving accident and emergency cases should be in the centre of the district it served. This usually meant a congested city or town centre site, with little room for subsequent expansion. Moreover, some sites which were convenient when the hospitals were first built had become inappropriate by reason of population movements. On the other hand, most mental hospitals had been deliberately built on secluded sites out in the country, and by 1948 not only was this giving rise to problems of staffing, but the wisdom of thus segregating the mentally ill was being questioned.

THE NHS INHERITANCE

The Hospital Surveys carried out during the Second World War by the Ministry of Health and the Nuffield Provincial Hospitals Trust working in collaboration focused attention on these and other problems which stemmed from the fact that in the twentieth century hospital building had not – in spite of the vigorous growth of the voluntary hospitals in the 1930s – kept pace with medical, social and demographic change.

In the North Western Area, for example, the ministry's surveyors noted that:

> Generally speaking, it must be recognised that the existing hospitals, considered as buildings, fall far short of a satisfactory standard. Indeed, considering the high place which England takes in the medical world, perhaps the most striking thing about them is how bad they are. This is less surprising, however, when one realises how old they are. The number of new hospitals built during this century is surprisingly small and the number built in the inter-war period very small indeed.

The North Western Area, comprising Cumberland, Westmorland, Lancashire, Cheshire and North Wales, had been the cradle of the Industrial Revolution and had suffered much during the Depression, so it was perhaps a particularly bad case, but surveyors in several other areas were equally critical. On the other hand, the same surveyors observed that not only did the voluntary hospitals commonly serve both the town in which they were situated and some surrounding area of countryside, but county and county borough councils had frequently made arrangements for their hospitals to serve areas which did not coincide with local government boundaries but represented a response to demography and the availability of transport.

Often hospitals had squeezed additional wards and departments on to restricted sites, creating difficult working conditions and detracting from any efficiency the original layout might have had. Some former Poor Law hospitals had changed from the care of the chronic sick to the provision of acute hospital services, and in many cases their buildings simply were not suitable for this new type of work.

The outbreak of the Second World War brought hospital building virtually to a standstill. The Emergency Medical Service added some 50,000 beds to existing hospitals, but these were mostly in buildings intended to be temporary and they were not necessarily where additional beds needed to be for peacetime purposes. A further consequence of the war was that routine maintenance of existing buildings was neglected and many of the older hospitals ended the war in a fairly advanced state of dilapidation.

There remained the question of whether – whatever the state of the buildings in which they were housed – the country had enough hospital beds for its needs. The 1937 PEP *Report on the British Health Services* concluded that there was a real and at times a serious shortage of hospital beds in Great Britain, although analysis of the long waiting lists of some hospitals had shown that the shortage was not as bad as it appeared, and in an emergency a bed was always found. The problem was at least to some extent one of using existing beds to better advantage, rather than making good an absolute shortage.

Similar notes of caution were to be found in the Hospital Surveys. For instance, the surveyors for London and the surrounding area reported:

> In general, there can be little doubt that in quantity or in quality or both, hospital accommodation is deficient in every area, and a very large building programme will be needed to raise the standard to an adequate level. In many areas, however, wartime extensions of the Emergency Hospital Scheme will provide relief at least of a temporary

kind; and in London itself (apart from the southern fringe of the county) it may be increasingly found that there is too much accommodation rather than too little. For these reasons it seems to us that the question of hospital building must be approached with circumspection.

EARLY YEARS OF THE NHS

In the early years of the NHS, the question of hospital building was indeed approached with circumspection, although perhaps dictated more by national economic problems and the relatively high priority the government were giving to the building of schools and houses than by any sense that there was a danger of providing too many hospital beds. The small amount of money available for hospital building in the first few years – rising from £8·7 million in 1949/50 to £9·8 million in 1954/5 – was chiefly spent on work that would add to the efficiency of existing hospitals, such as the addition of new operating theatres, the expansion of outpatient facilities, or the improvement of diagnostic departments. It was estimated that in these years the level of capital investment was only about one-fifth of that which prevailed in the years immediately before the war. In 1955 part of the capital allocation was for the first time earmarked for schemes costing over £250,000 so as to allow major reconstruction and the building of new hospitals to begin. About the same time money was also set aside for the improvement of psychiatric hospitals, many of which were still dismal and forbidding places. The sums spent on hospital building then rose from £10·6 million in 1955/6 to £23·7 million in 1960/1. This latter figure must be set against the estimate produced for the 1956 Guillebaud Committee that an annual expenditure of £30 million would be required merely to keep pace with the depreciation of existing hospital buildings, if sixty years was considered to be an appropriate span of life for a hospital. If buildings were to be depreciated over ninety years then £20 million would be the annual expenditure required at 1956 values. Clearly Britain's hospitals were not only old and in bad shape, they were becoming more dilapidated every day.

Meanwhile, although few hospitals were actually being built, the Nuffield Provincial Hospitals Trust were making an important contribution to hospital design with a series of research studies directed by Richard (later Lord) Llewelyn-Davies and John Weeks. The Nuffield team recommended a clean break with the traditional Nightingale ward design of a long room with beds down either side and little privacy for the patients other than that which could be afforded by movable screens placed temporarily round a bed. They suggested 20–25 per cent of the beds should be in single rooms for very ill patients or patients who for reasons of infection or otherwise were best nursed away from others. The remaining beds were grouped in four or six bed bays. The studies which led up to these recommendations had stressed the reduction of walking distances for nurses, and ease of supervision. Between 1955 and the early 1960s wards based on Nuffield designs were built at Larkfield Hospital, Greenock, Musgrave Park Hospital, Belfast, and at Swindon.

THE HOSPITAL PLAN

In 1962 the publication by the Ministry of Health of *A Hospital Plan for England and Wales* gave the architects and planners their opportunity. By 1971 the government planned to have spent £500 million on building ninety new hospitals and modernising and extending existing hospitals. The Plan was based on a comprehensive review, region by region, of the country's hospitals and on a series of estimates of the appropriate ratios of beds to population in the main specialities. For acute beds the recommended ratio was 3·3/1,000 (compared with existing provision of 3·9/1,000); maternity beds 0·58/1,000 (0·45/1,000); geriatric beds 1·4/1,000 (1·5/1,000); mental illness beds 1·8/1,000 (3·3/1,000); mental subnormality beds 1·3/1,000 (1·3/1,000). Clearly the ministry felt the country had too many hospital beds overall – although the existing ratios concealed wide regional variations – and that with the exception of maternity and mental subnormality what was required was fewer beds but of a better standard, in the right places, and better used. As far as general hospitals were concerned the proposal was that a smaller number of rather larger hospitals could better serve the needs of the population than the existing patchwork of small and medium-sized hospitals. The total number of hospital beds would decrease from around 470,000 to 430,000, and some 1,250 hospitals, many of them small, would close. The recommended ratios of beds to population were to some extent arbitrary. It was clear from experience in some regions that patients did not need to stay in hospital as long as they often did, and if they were discharged earlier fewer beds would be required. Some areas were managing on as few as 2·0 acute beds per 1,000 population without any obvious detriment to the health of the population served. The ratio of 3·3/1,000 was therefore a fairly cautious estimate.

The district general hospital
The basis of the Plan was the district general hospital of 600–800 beds serving a population of 100,000–150,000 and providing treatment and diagnostic facilities for both inpatients and outpatients in all the com-

moner specialities. This was a concept that had been described in some detail the previous year in the third of the series of Building Notes produced by the ministry's hospital research and development group. In the district general hospital there would be some mental illness beds and a geriatric unit, although separate provision away from the district general hospital would still be required in these specialities. Some of the more highly specialised units (e.g. neurosurgery, plastic surgery) would be provided only at selected district general hospitals and would normally serve a region or a sub-regional area.

The idea of the district general hospital can be traced back to the wartime Hospital Surveys. In the London survey, the authors, Mr A. M. H. Gray and Dr A. Topping, wrote:

> The foundation stone of the hospital service is the specialist hospital referred to in these recommendations as a District Hospital, that is an acute general hospital staffed by specialists and assistants and providing for all normal types of acute work both out-patient and in-patient . . . Ideally there should be one such District Hospital in each district of convenient size and population, and it should include a block for the chronic sick, a separate maternity unit, and in many areas a separate fever block . . . The size of the District Hospital will vary according to the local circumstances, but it should probably not much exceed 1,000 beds or fall below 400, with the optimum at about 800. This would serve an area with a population of between one and two hundred thousand.

Justifying the proposed rationalisation of hospital services the 1962 Hospital Plan argued:

> In recent years there has been a trend towards greater interdependence of the various branches of medicine and also an increasing realisation of the need to bring together a wide range of the facilities required for diagnosis and treatment . . . The district general hospital offers the most practicable method of placing the full range of hospital facilities at the disposal of patients and this consideration far outweighs the disadvantage of longer travel for some patients and their visitors.

Not all patients and their visitors agreed that this was so, and there was to be opposition over the years to the closure of small hospitals in areas where travel was difficult for those without cars or where local sentiment was strongly attached to a small hospital which had served its district well. None the less the Plan did not suggest a clean sweep of all small hospitals. Many would still be needed; some would be retained as maternity units, although any new maternity beds would be provided at the district general hospital; others would become long-stay geriatric units. Some small hospitals in remote areas, or in isolated towns receiving large numbers of visitors in the summer, would even continue to admit acute cases that did not require specialist facilities.

Maternity beds

The recommendation in the Plan for an increased number of maternity beds reflected the 1959 recommendation of the Cranbrook Committee on Maternity Services that 70 per cent of confinements should take place in hospital, compared with 60 per cent in the mid-1950s, and also the rising birth rate (15 per 1,000 in 1955 rising to 18·5 per 1,000 in 1964, but thereafter declining to 13·8 by 1973). However, by the time the Peel Committee on Domiciliary Midwifery and Maternity Bed Needs reported in 1970, well over 80 per cent of deliveries were taking place in hospitals and the Committee felt confident that with the lower birth rate and the shorter stays in hospital that had by then become customary a ratio of 0·5 maternity beds per 1,000 population would allow their goal of 100 per cent hospital confinement to be achieved.

Mental illness beds

The most drastic reduction proposed in the Hospital Plan was in respect of mental illness, from 3·3/1,000 to 1·8/1,000 – a cut of 45 per cent. This was based on the belief that with new methods of treatment and changed social attitudes towards the mentally ill the reduction that had been experienced in beds required for the mentally ill during the previous few years would continue. It was even felt that with expansion of community mental health services and possible further advances in treatment the ratio of 1·8/1,000 might by 1975 be too high. The statistical projections on which the Hospital Plan relied envisaged that 0·9 beds per 1,000 might in the future be needed for patients staying less than two years, and a further 0·9 per 1,000 for new long-stay patients. It was assumed that none of the 110,000 long-stay patients in mental hospitals in 1960 would still be there by 1975, but this assumption proved to be somewhat wide of the mark. By the early 1970s the number of beds used for patients staying less than two years and for newly arising long-stay patients were close to the General Register Office projections, but the rate of discharge of the original long-stay population had flattened out considerably, and some 30,000 of the original 110,000 were still in hospital. As many of these were still under 65 it was plain that they would have to be accommodated for many years to come.

The expected reduction in bed ratios and the policy of siting units for short-stay psychiatric patients in district general hospitals meant, according to the Hospital Plan, that a large number of existing mental hospitals would within fifteen years become redundant and close. There was thus concern among mental hospital staffs that their jobs were on the one hand threatened and on the other would become less interesting as the acute work was concentrated in the district general hospitals and those mental hospitals that remained open became dumping grounds for patients who had been designated as virtually incurable. Morale only started to recover when it became clear, first, that more intensive methods of treatment required more staff for fewer patients and that the district general hospitals would be looking to the mental hospitals to staff their acute psychiatric units, and secondly, that the rate at which it would be possible to run down and close existing mental hospitals had been overestimated.

So it was that the future role of the large mental hospital was still a live issue when the NHS was reorganised in 1974. Indeed, two years after that reorganisation the King's Fund held a conference on that very theme, and the views expressed ranged from a belief that it was possible to practise psychiatry without buildings to the claim that the traditional mental hospital was the ideal site for the treatment of a wide range of patients. But in 1961, even before publication of the Hospital Plan, the minister, Enoch Powell, had no doubts:

> Psychiatric patients ought for the most part to be in wards and wings of general hospitals. Few ought to be in great isolated institutions or clumps of institutions, though I neither forget nor underestimate the continuing requirements of security for a small minority of patients.
>
> Now look and see what are the implications of these bold words. They imply nothing less than the elimination of by far the greater part of this country's mental hospitals as they exist today. This is a colossal undertaking, not so much in the new physical provision which it involves, as in the sheer inertia of mind and matter which it requires to be overcome. There they stand, isolated, majestic, imperious, brooded over by the gigantic water-tower and chimney combined, rising unmistakable and daunting out of the countryside – the asylums which our forefathers built with such immense solidity to express the notions of their day. Do not for a moment underestimate their powers of resistance to our assault.

THE COMMUNITY CARE PLAN

Publication of the Hospital Plan was followed closely by *Health and Welfare: the Development of Community Care*, an aggregation by the Ministry of Health of local authorities' proposals for the development of their health and welfare services. No attempt was made to indicate to local authorities what standards of provision they should be aiming at. RHB's proposals for hospital building had been carefully vetted and at times substantially modified by the ministry, but no such process was followed with the local authorities. None the less in many respects the Hospital Plan had been based on the assumption that community services would develop in such a way as to enable many patients to be cared for in the community who had previously been likely to occupy a hospital bed. For instance, the ratio of 10 geriatric beds per 1,000 population over the age of 65 (1·4 per 1,000 total population) assumed that the standard of services for the elderly outside hospital would be brought generally up to the level of the best current practice.

Health and Welfare: the Development of Community Care showed that the 146 local health and welfare authorities of England and Wales were planning by 1972 to build more than 1,000 new residential homes for the elderly, and more than 1,000 training centres, homes and hostels for the physically and mentally handicapped and the mentally ill, at a cost of well over £200 million. A 45 per cent increase in staff was envisaged. The ministry's introductory comment drew attention to the change of emphasis from the provision of particular services to the meeting of particular needs, and the fifty-page text (which was followed by 320 pages of statistical tables setting out the local authorities' plans in detail) was organised in chapters based on the needs of four broad groups: mothers and young children; the elderly; the mentally disordered; and the physically handicapped; followed by chapters on other groups in need of community care; on the ambulance service; and on voluntary effort.

There were wide variations between authorities, but some general trends were apparent. A surprising number of authorities were planning to increase the number of domiciliary midwives at a time when the number of home deliveries was falling. The figure of 6,509 whole-time equivalents which the local authorities' plans envisaged by 1972 represented a 15 per cent increase. In the event, by the end of 1971 authorities were employing 28 per cent fewer midwives. The ministry thought local authority estimates of the numbers of health visitors they would require were on the low side. The plans envisaged an increase from 5,213 whole-time equivalents in 1961 to 7,607 by 1972 and the ministry thought the figure ought to have been around 8,600. In the event the local authorities did not even achieve the target they had set themselves, with only 6,053 whole-time equivalents by the end of 1971. The local authority plans hardly mentioned health centres. There were seventeen already in existence, plans for four more were at an advanced stage, and twenty-six more were proposed to be built by 1972. Within the next few years the situation had changed completely, doctors were increasingly keen to work in health centres and local authorities to provide them. By 1972 there were more than 240 health centres in England and Wales, and by the time the NHS was reorganised there were some 500.

It was envisaged that both the Hospital Plan and the local authorities' plans would be revised and carried forward at frequent intervals. A revision of the Hospital Plan was published in 1966 and revisions of the Plan for Community Care in 1964 and 1966. By the time the Hospital Plan was revised in 1966 the ministry had accumulated enough experience to realise that hospitals were not being built as quickly as they had hoped would be possible, and they were costing rather more than had been expected. The original Plan had said that building standards and cost limits would be laid down to govern all future hospital building and that the possibility of reaping economies through standardisation was being explored. The ministry's experience of the first few years of the hospital building programme not only compelled revision of the original cost limits, but gave additional impetus to efforts to achieve savings through standardisation and increasingly strict control over the space and facilities to be provided in each new hospital.

DEVELOPMENTS IN HOSPITAL DESIGN

In the 1960s there was a good deal of experimentation in hospital design. In addition to hospitals built on the Nuffield planning principles (see above), there were hospitals influenced by American designs, either in terms of their general configuration (e.g. high-rise ward block sitting on a podium which housed diagnostic, service and outpatient departments) or in terms of internal ward layout (e.g. the 'racetrack' ward with patients' rooms arranged around a central core of service rooms). The firm of Llewelyn-Davies, Weeks and Partners were developing the concept of the 'indeterminate hospital', designed to grow and change without disruption of its basic communication pattern, and the ministry's own architect's department were experimenting at Greenwich with a design that managed to pack 800 beds on to a restricted urban site without going more than three storeys high. This was achieved by spending the money that was saved through not going high on complete air conditioning, unusual in British hospitals at this date.

RHBs all had their own architect's departments, although they varied in the proportion of their projects that they tackled themselves and the proportion they commissioned private architects to design on their behalf. Several RHBs were developing their own systems for standardising hospital building and thus cutting costs. Leeds RHB produced a

design for a 600-bed general hospital, known as PGH600, which was
built first at Airedale and then, outside the region, in South Cheshire.
It was claimed to cost only £7,000 per bed at a time when other hospitals
were costing £10,000. The ministry architects drew both on their own
experience at Greenwich and on the Leeds PGH600 design to produce
what was described as the 'Best Buy' hospital. Conceived in the mid-
1960s, this was subsequently built at Bury St Edmunds in Suffolk and
at Frimley, Surrey. Most hospitals were then being built in phases, as
money became available, but the 'Best Buy' was designed to be built
in one phase as a hospital of 500–600 beds. Simple in construction and
limited to two storeys making maximum use of natural light and ventila-
tion, it was intended also to effect economies by providing only the
minimum number of beds for its district, on the assumption that
community services would be fully developed to enable as many patients
as possible to be cared for at home, and those who were admitted to
hospital to be discharged quickly. In the Mark I version of 'Best Buy'
space requirements were cut so drastically that the working of the
hospital was impaired, and Mark II was therefore designed on slightly
more generous lines.

THE BONHAM-CARTER REPORT

In 1969 there was published the Report of the Committee on the
Functions of the District General Hospital (Bonham-Carter Report),
which was set up by the Central Health Services Council after the
Council had been addressed by Professor T. McKeown, professor of
social medicine at the University of Birmingham. McKeown had for
some years been arguing the case for what he termed the 'balanced
hospital community'. The Bonham-Carter Report was heavily influenced by his views and urged the integration of hospital psychiatric and
geriatric services on the same site and under the same administration
as the acute medical and surgical facilities. McKeown's argument was
that any other solution, such as the partial integration envisaged in the
original Hospital Plan, was to condemn psychiatric and geriatric
patients to second-class facilities and second-class care.

The Bonham-Carter Report also suggested that district general
hospitals should be rather larger than the 600–800 beds described in the
Plan. An increase in size was of course implied in the full integration
of psychiatry and geriatrics, but the clinching argument for the Committee was one relating to medical staffing. The view was accepted that
no consultant should work on his own, and thus without frequent
contact with colleagues in the same specialty and without cover at
consultant level when off duty or absent, and that ideally no consultant

in an acute specialty should be in charge of inpatients at more than one hospital. It followed that for each acute specialty catered for in a district general hospital there ought to be at least two consultants, with appropriate supporting staff. Specialties such as orthopaedic surgery and paediatrics could hardly justify two consultants for a hospital serving only 100,000–150,000 population, so it was necessary to think in terms of larger hospitals serving bigger populations. The Report suggested hospitals of 1,000–1,750 beds serving populations of 200,000–300,000.

The Bonham-Carter Committee accepted that some small hospitals in peripheral areas from which it was difficult to reach the district general hospital should be retained, but felt these should only undertake work that could be considered within the scope of local general practitioners, without resident junior medical staff or more than occasional visits from consultants and specialists.

The government gave only a lukewarm reception to the Bonham-Carter Report, and in 1971 the Department of Health asked RHBs not to plan district general hospitals larger than 750–1,100 beds, but in due course Sir Keith Joseph, who succeeded Richard Crossman as Secretary of State when Labour were defeated in the 1971 election, indicated how far he was prepared to go in the direction the Report had indicated. 'One foundation of the new National Health Service', he said – discussions and consultations on reorganisation were by then well under way – 'will be on the hospital side, the district general hospitals, each providing comprehensive services for populations up to about 250,000 people. There will be something like 230 of them. Perhaps three-quarters of them will have more than 600 beds and the 1,000-bed hospital will not be uncommon.' But he went on to explain that he had been taking a careful look at the place of the local hospital in the scheme of things:

> I am a healthy sceptic of over-centralisation and there *will* be local hospitals. The Government sees the need for what we are now calling community hospitals – for patients who need hospital care but do not need all the expensive facilities of a district general hospital. In these local hospitals they can be looked after nearer their homes and friends, benefiting from the goodwill and service, whether voluntary or paid, that can be focused on a small hospital serving its local community.

Criticism of the Bonham-Carter concept of the very large district general hospital had centred on the, it was said, excessive weight that had been attached to considerations of medical staffing, the difficulties of managing such very large organisations, and doubts on the part of economists as to whether the hoped-for economies of scale would be realised. In addition, however, the hospital building programme could not be revised at short notice to take account of the Bonham-Carter recommendations, even had they been wholeheartedly accepted by the government, as many hospitals were already under construction or at an advanced design stage. By the time the next generation of hospitals were being designed the financial difficulties that the hospital building programme was then experiencing made it extremely doubtful whether such very large projects could be contemplated.

PROBLEMS WITH THE HOSPITAL BUILDING PROGRAMME

Meanwhile the search for more economical methods of hospital design and construction continued. Towards the end of the 1960s the Department of Health tried to draw together the various initiatives that had been taken by RHBs in what became known as the 'Harness' programme. Whereas 'Best Buy' was a standard hospital, 'Harness' was a range of standard departments which could be combined in different ways in hospitals of from 600 to 800 beds. In the 'Harness' programme the opportunity was taken to update and improve the standards of provision set out in the earlier Ministry of Health Building Notes, with the result that by the time 'Harness' hospitals started to be built in the mid-1970s they represented a standard which the nation could no longer afford. This was the point at which the DHSS produced the 'Nucleus' concept, which drew on both 'Harness' and 'Best Buy', but which was intended to produce a hospital of a mere 300 beds, with variable functional content, capable of later expansion to 600–900 beds when needs dictated and money became available.

Anxiety over costs and the possibility of keeping them under effective control was a constant feature of the hospital building programme from its inception. The Ministry and Department of Health's attempts to promote a high degree of standardisation of components, layout and planning procedures reflected a desire not merely to avoid unnecessary costs, but to make it possible to predict accurately what a given scheme would in fact cost. These efforts met with only limited success. The department's own 'Best Buy' schemes at Bury St Edmunds and Frimley incurred the censure of the Public Accounts Committee because in each case about 3,000 detailed changes were made after the schemes went out to tender, with resultant additional costs. In 1973 the department had the embarrassment of receiving a report commissioned from a construction industry expert, H. J. Cruickshank, on the planning, design and construction of hospital buildings, in which it was stated: 'it is of course axiomatic that any system of standardisation, particularly on the national scale envisaged, will produce hospital buildings whose capital construction costs will be higher than those for traditional designed buildings'. Originally it was hoped that the hospital building programme would reap some of the economies and other advantages from standardisation that had accrued in the building of schools in the 1950s, but hospital buildings – in which from 35 to 55 per cent of costs may be accounted for by engineering services – are inherently more complex than schools, and in the design of a hospital it is usually felt necessary to take into account the views of the professional staff who will in future work in the buildings under consideration to an extent which seldom applies elsewhere.

An accelerating rate of monetary inflation added to the difficulties of the hospital building programme. At times the capacity of the construction industry appeared to be stretched, but it was alleged that the failure of more than one large and previously prosperous firm could be traced to its having taken on a hospital project. Firms complained of cumbersome planning procedures, frequent and late changes of mind on the part of the client authorities, reluctance to pay the full costs of additional work, and late payment of accounts. British hospitals took longer to plan, design and build than was the case in almost any other country. When in 1968 the Spaniards planned, built and opened a 1,100-bed general hospital in Valencia in only eighteen months, British hospital architects marvelled; in Britain a comparable project would have taken ten years. Hospital board architects who visited newly built continental hospitals also looked enviously at the standard of fittings and finishes, designed to make subsequent maintenance trouble-free and cheap. Tight cost limits all too often meant that British hospitals were shoddily finished and incurred high maintenance costs in subsequent years.

The proportion of the health budget that was spent on capital schemes rose steadily. The proportion of capital money spent on very large schemes also rose. Defining a large scheme as one in which building is proceeding at the rate of more than £1 million a year, 1968 was the first year in which large schemes accounted for more than half the spending on capital account. There were sixty nine such schemes in progress during the year, and six of them were planned to cost over £10 million each by the time they were completed. Capital expenditure expressed as a percentage of current expenditure amounted in that year to 9·9 per cent, and over the next few years it rose steadily to the peak of 12·8 per cent in 1973/4. In the first year of the reorganised NHS, 1974/5, it was pulled sharply back to 9·9 per cent and the future building programme was cut drastically to allow the government to estimate a further reduction to 7·1 per cent by 1979/80. It was Dr David Owen, Minister of State for Health from 1974 to 1977, who later wrote: 'the hospital building programme in 1972–3, like so much public expenditure in this country . . . was completely out of control. Even if Britain had been able to sustain its then rate of economic expansion the forward planning of hospitals was completely unrealistic'.

Part of the trouble was inflation – a scheme estimated to cost £5 million might cost more than twice that in depreciated money by the time it was completed. Then the new hospitals were inevitably much more expensive to run than the old ones, not because they were necessarily less efficiently planned – the reverse would usually have been the case – but because rebuilding to the same standard would simply not have been acceptable, and higher standards cost more in terms of space, engineering services, staff etc. Again, as the pay of hospital staff improved substantially in the early 1970s the cost implications of higher levels of staffing became that much more serious.

The fact that the Department of Health underwrote the additional running costs of new buildings and hospitals, and subsequently health, authorities did not have to find the extra money out of their normal allocations had a distorting effect on the attempts that were being made to close the gap between regions that had always been relatively well funded and those that had always had relatively less. A region opening a number of new hospitals, or phases of hospitals, inevitably received extra money under the RCCS (revenue consequences of capital schemes) formula, even though the department might be planning to hold that region back in order to give extra to some less well endowed region. This was to lead to great difficulty two years after reorganisation when the government of the day made renewed and rather more determined efforts to correct traditional inequalities between different regions and between areas within regions.

THE COMMUNITY HOSPITAL

By the time the NHS was reorganised the 'community hospital', as Sir Keith Joseph had called it, had emerged as an important theme. It harmonised with the by then widespread distrust of large construction contracts and big remote hospitals, it was a suitably modest theme for a time of economic stringency, and the community hospital was expected to set aside two-thirds or more of its beds for the elderly, including elderly patients with dementia, thus making an important contribution to a field which was then being given a high priority in government pronouncements. The remaining beds would be used largely for medical patients who might otherwise need a bed in a district general hospital, or for surgical patients transferred early from the district hospital, thus making it possible to use district hospital beds more intensively.

The community hospital idea had been pioneered in the Oxford Region in the late 1960s, well before Sir Keith Joseph used the phrase. It developed from a study of the work of the cottage hospital at Chipping Norton and consideration of ways in which the scope of such hospitals could be extended to bring relief to the district general hospitals and to cut travelling distances for patients and their relatives. The first purpose-built community hospital opened at Wallingford in 1973, but it was clear that for many years the majority of community hospitals would be created by adaptation and review of the functions of existing buildings.

At the outset of the NHS, Aneurin Bevan had declared that although he was not a devotee of bigness for bigness' sake, 'I would rather be kept alive in the efficient if cold altruism of a large hospital than expire in a gush of warm sympathy in a small one'. The district general hospital paid tribute to the technological complexity of modern medicine, but the community hospital was a reassertion of the values of smallness and proximity, and perhaps too a concession to the view that it would never be possible to care in their own homes for all the patients who on strict medical indications did not 'need' a hospital bed.

5
Pandora's Box – Sans Everything and After

In my early days there I heard a charge nurse snarl at an old man lying in bed: 'Die, you bastard, die.' The old man replied: 'It takes time, Charge.' 'Nobody Wants To Know', from *Sans Everything*

Speaking in a House of Commons debate in February 1954, Kenneth Robinson, a Labour Member who had been keenly interested in mental health questions for a number of years, and who subsequently became Minister of Health, painted a grim picture of the nation's mental hospitals. Overcrowding was rife, with patients' beds frequently only nine inches apart, and some patients sleeping on beds in the corridors. An average length of stay was a statistical fallacy. What was happening was that in a small number of beds in acute or admission units patients were being treated intensively and discharged after a few weeks. The rest of the beds were filled by patients who stayed for many years. The buildings were old and barrack-like, there was a grave shortage of nurses and the atmosphere was institutional in the extreme. Yet mental hospitals accounted for 42 per cent of the nation's stock of hospital beds. The then Minister of Health had allocated a million pounds to be spent on improving mental hospitals in the coming year, the first time such a sum had been earmarked in this way, but Kenneth Robinson declared that this was 'a drop in the ocean. We want many, many millions, and we want them urgently.'

Replying to this debate – in which Members had also drawn attention to the wide disparity between the average cost of keeping a patient in a mental hospital for a week (£4 6s 7d) and the cost of a week in a general hospital (£13 13s 6d) – the Parliamentary Secretary to the Ministry of

Health, Miss Pat Hornsby-Smith, agreed that existing buildings were 'an appalling legacy', which would cost thousands of millions of pounds over many years to replace, but observed that one cause of the overcrowding was that people were living longer, and this increased the number of psychogeriatric patients. People were also coming forward more readily to be treated for mental illness on a voluntary basis.

DEVELOPMENTS IN MENTAL HEALTH CARE

This debate was the curtain-raiser to the deliberations of the Royal Commission on the Law Relating to Mental Illness and Mental Deficiency (the Percy Commission), the appointment of which had been announced the previous October. When the Percy Report was published in 1957 it suggested important changes in the legal framework within which mental health services were provided. The Mental Health Act of 1959, which implemented many of the Royal Commission's recommendations, introduced a new terminology. 'Mental disorder' was used to embrace both mental illness and mental handicap, and the four recognised categories of patients suffering from mental disorder became the mentally ill, the mentally subnormal, the severely subnormal, and the psychopathic. (Mental handicap is a term which came into use among the professions in the 1960s as one which was thought to be less stigmatising than mental subnormality, although the latter remained the term that had to be employed in legal contexts.) All existing legislation on mental disorder and its treatment was repealed and provisions were made that mental disorder should as far as possible be treated, administratively, in the same way as physical illness and with no more formality, except in those cases in which compulsory admission could be shown to be essential. Procedures for compulsory admission, where this was still necessary, were streamlined, as were the arrangements for the discharge of detained patients. Mental health tribunals were set up in each area to review individual cases. The Act represented a move away from legalism in the care of the mentally disordered and was designed to reduce stigma and encourage early treatment.

At the same time, important developments in clinical psychiatry were taking place. The introduction in the early 1950s of the phenothiazine group of drugs made it possible to control disturbed behaviour without the locked doors and close supervision that had previously been necessary. Many patients could now be treated in the community or as day patients instead of being kept in hospital. It became a matter of pride in a mental hospital to have no or few locked doors, and the term 'open door policy' referred both to this and to the ease with which patients were, after 1959, admitted and discharged. For some patients the open door became a revolving door as they had to be readmitted following a relapse or a failure to adjust to life in the community. None the less it was held to be an advance if a patient spent even some months each year in the community, rather than all his life in the hospital. It was only possible to dispute this in those cases where the behaviour of patients imposed intolerable burdens on their families while they were out of hospital.

The drive to get patients, especially long-stay patients, out of hospital received additional impetus from the publication in the same year as the new Mental Health Act of Dr Russell Barton's book *Institutional Neurosis*. It had often been assumed that the apathy, loss of individuality, and automaton-like behaviour seen in mental hospital patients was an inevitable result of their illness, but Barton showed that this condition was essentially caused by the institutional regime to which the patients were subjected, interacting perhaps with the original mental illness, but having much in common with personality changes that had been observed in prisons and other settings in which there was loss of contact with the outside world. Earlier writers had used such terms as 'prison stupor' and 'psychological institutionalism', but it was Barton's term that achieved wide currency, although it was to some extent later superseded by the more general term 'institutionalisation', as used by sociologists such as Goffman (who applied it to schools, prisons and other institutional settings as well as mental hospitals). By then it was recognised that staff, as well as patients, became institutionalised and lost the ability to break out of routine patterns of behaviour and take new initiatives. Several of the reports arising from official inquiries into conditions and happenings in mental hospitals and long-stay hospitals for the elderly from 1967 onwards could be regarded as case studies in institutional neurosis or the sociology of closed institutions.

Most, though of course not all, long-stay patients in hospitals for the physically ill were elderly, and in due course many hospitals known in 1948 as hospitals for the chronic sick became known as geriatric hospitals. The change of title might or might not be accompanied by any marked change in regime or circumstances. There was, as there always had been, overlap between the elderly patients cared for in mental hospitals because they were supposed to be, or once had been, mentally disturbed, and those who were cared for in chronic sick or geriatric hospitals because of a physical infirmity that might well be accompanied by a degree of mental disorientation. Hospitals for the chronic sick traditionally had fewer nurses in proportion to the number of patients than other hospitals, and usually a smaller proportion of the nurses would be qualified. Yet it had always been a particularly demanding branch of nursing. The scant resources allocated to long-stay hospitals reflected not the needs of the patients so much as their status. No one ever actually said, 'What is the point of spending a great deal of money on them ?', but most nurses and doctors found more satisfaction in caring for the acutely ill, who might get better, than for patients who it was assumed would need care for the rest of their days. It was left to a handful of dedicated geriatricians and nurses to show what could be done for many of these patients if hope were not prematurely abandoned, but the environment in which they worked militated most powerfully against their efforts. Old buildings, many still bearing the stigma of the Poor Law, frequently geographically as well as professionally isolated; poor standards of equipment; low levels of staffing and a high ratio of unqualified staff, were among the handicaps they had to overcome. With the elderly, as with the mentally ill, the conventional wisdom was that whenever possible they should be cared for in the community; at best in their own homes, otherwise in a home provided by the local welfare authority, rather than a hospital. However, even though the considerable majority even of infirm old people were cared for by their families in their own homes, some had no families, some had no homes, and local authorities seldom provided enough places in welfare homes to meet the potential demand.

'SANS EVERYTHING'

This point was taken up by Lord Strabolgi when he spoke in a debate on community care in the House of Lords in July 1966. Many old people were admitted to mental hospitals, he said, not because they were mentally ill, but because there was nowhere else for them to go. Most of these mental hospitals were good, but some were a disgrace to a civilised country, and old people in them were treated worse than in the old-fashioned type of Victorian workhouse. 'There is, for example', he went on, 'the practice of what is known as "stripping". This means that on entry all personal belongings are removed, including spectacles, deaf aids and dentures. There are no personal lockers. The food is appalling. In some cases the last meal is served at half past three in the afternoon.' Lord Strabolgi spoke of hospitals in which patients had nothing to do, and no effort was made to find something to interest them. They hardly saw a doctor from one year's end to another. The nursing staff did their best, but they were overworked, which led to lack of attention, and sometimes even to cruelty.

In the previous year Lord Strabolgi had joined forces with Mrs Barbara Robb to found Aid for the Elderly in Government Institutions (AEGIS), and they had been two of the signatories of a letter to *The Times* which spoke out powerfully about the way old people were treated in many hospitals, general as well as mental. As a result of this letter, and of a letter written by another of the signatories, the Very Rev. Daniel Woolgar OP, to the *Catholic Herald*, a number of nurses and social workers, as well as members of the general public, wrote to AEGIS making in many cases extremely detailed allegations about the care of the elderly in particular institutions. Some of these cases were then put together in a book, edited by Barbara Robb for AEGIS and published in 1967 under the title *Sans Everything: A Case to Answer.*

In *Sans Everything* six nurses, two social workers and Mrs Robb herself described cases or conditions of which they claimed to have personal knowledge. Pseudonyms concealed the identity of the contributors (with the exception of Mrs Robb), the hospitals and the staff involved, although at a later stage the identities of the hospitals and of individuals involved were disclosed to the Committees of Inquiry that were set up to investigate the allegations made. The book had a Foreword by Dr Russell Barton, in which he pleaded that the disclosures which followed should not be made the ground for merely punitive measures against individuals. 'The one thing administrators, committees and many other people fail to learn', he wrote, 'is that kindness, pleasantness, sympathy and forbearance cannot be commanded by giving orders or passing resolutions. These qualities are to be found in 10 to 15 per cent of people regardless of the example they receive . . . For most people these qualities develop, or fail to develop, according to the example and manifest concern by senior staff.' While in a good hospital a high level of morale and team spirit would result in good standards of care, where standards were poor a misguided loyalty was likely to result in covering up and victimisation of anyone who voiced criticisms.

Other contributors to the book suggested steps that might bring about improvement. Among these, Professor Brian Abel-Smith suggested that on the analogy of the Parliamentary Commissioner (ombudsman) created by a recent Act, there should be set up a Hospital Commissioner, independent of the Ministry of Health and answerable only to Parliament. The Hospital Commissioner would have power to investigate those complaints he thought needed investigation and to act either on receipt of a complaint or on his own initiative, visiting hospitals unannounced and interviewing both patients and staff. He would not act as both prosecutor and judge, but would take those cases he decided to pursue before an independent tribunal which would be set up in each region and which, like the Commissioner, would be in no way part of the NHS.

After the publication of *Sans Everything*, the Minister of Health, Kenneth Robinson, asked the relevant hospital boards to appoint independent Committees of Inquiry into the allegations made against particular hospitals, and also to inquire into the present state of affairs in those hospitals. The findings of the six Committees of Inquiry that were then set up were published by HM Stationery Office in June 1968. The seven hospitals covered by the six inquiries were St James's Hospital, Leeds (a general hospital with many long-stay beds and a psychiatric unit); Storthes Hall Hospital, near Huddersfield (mental); Banstead Hospital, Sutton (mental); Cowley Road Hospital, Oxford (general, largely geriatric); Friern Hospital, London (mental); St Lawrence's Hospital, Bodmin (mental); and Springfield Hospital, Manchester (mental).

When the reports were published Kenneth Robinson made a statement to the House of Commons in which he said: 'These independent Committees of Enquiry find most of the allegations in *Sans Everything* to be totally unfounded or grossly exaggerated.' This was fair summary of those parts of the Reports which dealt purely with the specific allegations made in the book, but the minister went on to say: 'They make some criticisms of present conditions in the hospitals and suggest how they might be improved.' This was something of an understatement, particularly as far as the Report – considerably the most wide-ranging and detailed – on Friern Hospital was concerned. In examining 'the situation in the geriatric wards of Friern Hospital at the present time', the Committee painted a daunting picture of the difficulties under which staff were working and patients were being cared for. Much of the blame was laid at the door of the HMC and the RHB (the North West Metropolitan). The Committee concluded: 'principles have been ignored; and the remedy for consequential personal shortcomings lies in the study and application of sound principles of management, and not in personal recriminations.'

Many of the allegations in *Sans Everything* amounted to little more than lack of courtesy and consideration, a harsh word here and an unfeeling act there; and to say 'nothing more than' is not to imply that these things are not important, especially where the sick and helpless are concerned, but only to indicate how difficult it is to prove such things beyond reasonable doubt. The limitations of judicial inquiry into such matters were apparent in the six Reports. Those on Banstead, St James's, Storthes Hall and Springfield Hospitals were disturbingly short, summarising little of the evidence and presenting conclusions with an air of 'take it or leave it'. It was not surprising that the public were not wholly reassured. There was also the suspicion that Friern might not be an isolated case of mismanagement; that other hospitals up and down the country might be in a similar plight. Evidence was not long in coming that such was the case, but it was *Sans Everything* that first focused public attention on conditions in hospitals for the aged and the mentally ill and handicapped, which had been for so long starved both of resources and public interest. It thus enabled Richard Crossman – an energetic minister who succeeded Robinson when, in 1968, health was merged with social security and the post in charge of the combined department was given the rank of Secretary of State – to set in motion several measures designed to bring about improvement.

THE ELY HOSPITAL INQUIRY

However, publication of *Sans Everything* had been followed, in August 1967, by the publication in the *News of the World* of allegations made by a nursing assistant working at an unnamed hospital. The hospital subsequently transpired to be Ely Hospital, Cardiff. The *News of the World* had already forwarded the man's statement to the Minister of Health, who promptly set up a Committee of Inquiry under the chairmanship of Geoffrey Howe QC. The Committee's Report was published in 1969 and this time it not only criticised conditions at the hospital in a general way, but also supported many of the specific allegations of ill treatment and poor standards of care that 'XY', the nursing assistant, had made.

Ely Hospital was established in 1862 as a Poor Law Industrial School for Orphaned Children. In 1903 the school was transferred to an adjacent site, and Ely came to be used as a workhouse, housing the mentally ill, mentally defective, aged and infirm. In due course Ely was vested in the minister under the National Health Service Act 1946, and under the Mental Health Act 1959, Ely, by then accommodating a mixture of mentally ill and mentally subnormal patients – the latter much in the majority – was classified as a psychiatric hospital. From 1948 onwards Ely was administered first by the Whitchurch and Ely HMC and then, after a regrouping in 1965, by the Cardiff North and District HMC. It was interesting to note that since the start of the NHS Ely was in the same hospital group as Whitchurch Hospital, well known for progressive policies and high standards of care.

The Howe Report was highly critical of conditions at the hospital, of certain members of staff and senior officers, the HMC, the Welsh Hospital Board, and the general lack of effective provision for the supervision and inspection of hospitals such as Ely. Most of XY's allegations were upheld. 'Generally, the situation at Ely has proved to be sufficiently disturbing to make XY's concern well justified. It is a matter of speculation how long that situation would have persisted had it not been for XY's communication to the *News of the World*.'

The Report spoke of 'inertia', 'an unduly casual attitude towards death at Ely', 'the continued acceptance of old-fashioned, unduly rough and undesirably low standards of nursing care', of patients subjected to 'the unsophisticated technique of being slapped in the face', the 'low standard of medical care and record keeping in the male wards', and of the failure of 'basically good' men, the chief male nurse and the physician superintendent, to provide the necessary leadership and spur to improvement. A good deal of blame was laid on the 'isolation' – in professional rather than geographical terms – of Ely. Few staff were specifically trained in the care of the mentally subnormal, as distinct from the mentally ill, and there had been no opportunities provided for them to visit more progressive hospitals and acquire better standards. The physical conditions in this old, overcrowded hospital were daunting, and the Howe Committee made full allowance for this, but none the less found that standards of care fell short, not merely of the ideal, but of what ought to have been practicable in the circumstances, given good leadership.

The Report looked beyond the question of individual responsibility for standards of care at Ely to examine the role of the various levels of health service authority in this respect. The HMC, it was held, had not sufficiently appreciated their over-riding responsibility for standards of care, nor had they made themselves sufficiently aware of the problems of the hospital. On the other hand, since the minister was ultimately responsible there was a need for standards to be checked from time to time, on his behalf, by somebody who was not responsible for the day-to-day management of the hospital. This might have been the RHB (in Wales the Welsh Hospital Board), but many RHBs had interpreted early circulars expressing the minister's wish that HMCs should enjoy 'the maximum of autonomy' as precluding the regions from instituting any such system of inspection. Mental hospitals were until 1959 regularly inspected by the Board of Control, but this body was abolished by the Mental Health Act, and nothing had been set in its place.

During the *Sans Everything* furore, Kenneth Robinson had been reluctant to believe that any nurse would fear to come forward to provide evidence of ill treatment or neglect of patients. The *Nursing Mirror* obligingly asked its readers what they thought and the paper was overwhelmed with letters making it clear that there was a very real fear of victimisation. The Howe Report was able to document not only a fear of victimisation at Ely, but an actual case in which a nurse who had spoken out was dismissed even while the Committee of Inquiry was sitting. The nurse was only reinstated on appeal to the RHB, to whom the Howe Committee had submitted a report on his case.

THE HOSPITAL ADVISORY SERVICE

Following hard on the *Sans Everything* inquiries, the Howe Report added impetus to the setting up of the Hospital Advisory Service by the

Department of Health, and to the launching of a centrally sponsored training project designed to open up hospitals for the mentally subnormal to outside influences, where these had not previously been allowed to permeate, and to improve standards of care generally. The name of Ely became unhappily a byword for poor standards of care and neglect; unhappily because there were many staff who were doing their conscientious best in difficult circumstances, and also because after the publication of the Report the Welsh Hospital Board tried hard to improve both physical amenities and standards of care at the hospital. Staff understandably resented the difficulty they had in living down a bad name because of the widespread publicity the Report had received. The problem was to recur at other hospitals in the next few years. The role of RHBs was clarified by the issue of a DHSS circular emphasising their responsibilities to make themselves aware of standards of management and care in the hospitals within their regions.

The Hospital Advisory Service (HAS), set up as a body outside the Department of Health itself and reporting directly to the secretary of state, was conceived not strictly as an inspectorate. Its functions were laid down as:

(i) by constructive criticism and by propagating good practices and new ideas, to help to improve the management of patient care in individual hospitals (excluding matters of individual clinical judgement) and in the hospital service as a whole; and

(ii) to advise the Secretary of State for Social Services about conditions in hospitals in England and the Secretary of State for Wales about conditions in hospitals in Wales.

The HAS concentrated from the start on long-stay hospitals, although it was envisaged that its scope might eventually be extended to all NHS hospitals. Initially, however, a general hospital would only be visited if it had a geriatric or psychiatric unit. By the end of the first year, hospitals and departments with a total of 55,000 beds had been visited – some 12 per cent of the total number of hospital beds in the NHS. A visit by an HAS team would last from a few days to a week, and afterwards a report was sent to the Secretary of State, to the RHB, and to the HMC. These reports were not published, but the annual reports of the HAS discussed problems and trends in a general way, without naming individual hospitals.

FURTHER PROBLEMS AND INQUIRIES

In December 1968 the police were called to investigate allegations of ill treatment of patients by male nurses at Farleigh Hospital for the mentally handicapped, near Bristol, and as a result nine nurses were charged and convicted of offences under section 126(1)(a) of the Mental Health Act 1959. (This was the section that made it an offence for any member of a hospital staff to ill-treat or neglect a patient receiving treatment for mental disorder.) Two of the nurses were sent to prison for three years, the other, a nursing assistant, for two. As soon as the legal proceedings were ended a Committee of Inquiry began to consider the background to the offences.

Farleigh was, like Ely, a former Poor Law institution, still housed in its original 1838 building. North Ward, where difficult and potentially violent patients were concentrated, stood alone, separated from the other buildings by an open space surrounded by a high wooden fence. At the time, Farleigh had no hospital secretary, and no resident medical staff for its 270 patients. Administration was in the hands of the chief nurse, who was 'for all practical purposes . . . in complete and absolute control of the hospital'. Throughout the 1960s the senior psychiatrist was at loggerheads with the HMC, who attempted to remove much of his authority and to confer it on another doctor who was strictly the senior doctor's subordinate. This dispute robbed Farleigh of medical leadership; the chief nurse was overextended and overworked. The hospital failed to keep abreast of modern developments in the care of the mentally handicapped, and this failure went unrecognised by both the HMC and the RHB.

Less than two years after the events at Farleigh, two male nurses from Whittingham Hospital, Lancashire, were convicted of theft, and another male nurse, who attacked two patients, one of whom died, was convicted of manslaughter and imprisoned. In February 1971 the secretary of state set up the Payne Committee to inquire into Whittingham and its affairs. Again a number of serious allegations about the treatment of patients were upheld. The Committee were satisfied that allegations that patients received the 'wet towel treatment' – a wet towel was twisted round the patient's neck until he lost consciousness – when they were troublesome, and that methylated spirit was poured over patients' clothing and then set alight, were substantially true. They found that extensive pilfering of patients' money had taken place, and that this was made possible by the absence of any adequate system of financial control.

However, the way in which the hospital was run in general was severely criticised. 'Administration by labyrinth' was the telling phrase used in the Payne Report. The resignation of the HMC was called for, and indeed followed the inquiry. Among the suggestions made by the Payne Committee was that from day to day the hospital should be managed by a 'professional executive', consisting of the chairman of the medical staff, the chief nursing officer, the group secretary, and senior members of other professions working in the hospital. This system of management had been pioneered in the East Birmingham Hospital Group when James Elliott – a member of the Payne Committee – was group secretary. It was in due course adopted at Whittingham.

There was plenty of evidence that Whittingham was not essentially a bad hospital. Much good work was done, and many of the staff were devoted to their patients. But there were two standards of care, for the acute patients and the long-stay patients. Whittingham was 'a hospital of wide contrasts'. In the admission wards standards were good, but elsewhere there were many locked wards, with nurses brandishing large bunches of keys, and patients, in the words of the HMC chairman, 'sitting around all day just doing nothing but becoming cabbages'.

The 'two-tier' system of psychiatry, with much lower levels of staffing for the long-stay patients, had at least the tacit approval of the RHB, who were reluctant to admit that Whittingham was understaffed with psychiatrists. Manchester RHB had been foremost in developing the policy of attaching acute psychiatric units to general hospitals, as envisaged in the Hospital Plan (see Chapter 4), and considered Whittingham likely to close in fifteen to twenty years' time. This view, however, did not carry conviction with the HMC or the staff of the hospital, who saw a continuing need for Whittingham as a haven for long-stay patients who were unlikely ever to be discharged. These differences between the RHB and the HMC were never satisfactorily resolved, and there was thus a good deal of uncertainty and uneasiness among the staff. This appeared to the Payne Committee to be a fundamental cause of the hospital's malaise.

Progressive policies had unintended consequences elsewhere, too. In July 1972 fire swept through Winfrith Villa at Coldharbour Hospital, a hospital for the mentally handicapped at Sherborne, Dorset, and thirty patients lost their lives. Winfrith Villa had only recently been extensively refurnished, partitioned and improved to provide a more domestic atmosphere for the patients, but unhappily it had proved difficult to achieve this without using combustible materials. Had the authorities been content with a more institutional appearance, the fire might not have spread so rapidly and lives might not have been lost. The Report of the Committee of Inquiry set up as a result of the Coldharbour fire led to a heightened consciousness of the fire risks inherent in such improvement schemes, but the practical problems were not easy to solve.

At Napsbury Hospital, near St Albans, the problem was the enthusiastic application by a consultant psychiatrist of techniques which he believed to offer the best hope of returning certain long-stay schizophrenic patients to an independent life in the community. The methods pursued by Dr R. D. Scott involved the progressive withdrawal of nursing care and the handing over of responsibility for the ward environment to the patients themselves. By the time a series of complaints and untoward incidents prompted the secretary of state to set in motion what was on this occasion termed a 'professional investigation' rather than a Committee of Inquiry, Dr Scott's original treatment programme had been abandoned, partly as a consequence of reorganisation within the hospital which assigned to Dr Scott and his team responsibility for providing a total psychiatric service to a particular sector of the population served by the hospital. This was a form of organisation that was becoming increasingly common in psychiatric hospitals, but, as the report of the 'professional investigation' pointed out when it was published in 1973, it did not leave the consumer – the patient or his general practitioner – much choice of consultant. This might be a real problem where the consultant responsible for a sector held views and espoused methods of treatment with which many of his colleagues, and indeed members of the medical profession generally, disagreed. None the less this form of organisation commanded widespread support because it made for closer links between the hospital and the community it served.

'BETTER SERVICES FOR THE MENTALLY HANDICAPPED'

In 1971 the Department of Health published a White Paper, *Better Services for the Mentally Handicapped*, which proposed a major shift of emphasis, from hospitals to community care, in services for the mentally handicapped. It was suggested that the existing 52,100 hospital beds should in the long term be run down to little more than half that number as community services were developed. Hospitals should be used only for patients who required and could benefit from treatment. Those who simply required a home should be catered for by the local authority. Many of the principles laid down in the White Paper had been enunciated earlier by the Percy Commission, but while local authorities had in many cases developed a network of training centres for the mentally handicapped, they had still not built residential homes on the scale required if the hospital population was to be substantially reduced. As the White Paper put it, 'No new policy is involved for local authority services. What is needed is faster progress to overcome the present deficiencies.'

No new large hospitals for the mentally handicapped were to be built, and no hospital of more than 500 beds was to be enlarged. If more beds were required to relieve overcrowding in an existing hospital of more than 500 beds, then they were to be provided on another site. New inpatient accommodation would be provided either in special units within a general hospital or in separate hospitals of no more than 100–200 beds closely associated with a general hospital, even though not on the same site. New facilities for mentally handicapped children would normally be separate from those for adults, have close links with the children's department of a general hospital, and be provided in small domestic units. The White Paper also called on teaching hospitals to provide facilities for the mentally handicapped, both as part of their service to their districts, and so as to make future doctors familiar with the problems of mental handicap.

'BETTER SERVICES FOR THE MENTALLY ILL'

At the time the NHS was reorganised a parallel White Paper on *Better Services for the Mentally Ill* was in preparation. It was eventually published in October 1975. This White Paper also took as its theme a shift towards care in the community, but it spoke in cautious terms of the rundown of existing mental hospitals.

> The Government is, moreover, aware that both staff and patients and their families have felt that central authorities had not only failed to appreciate the pressures under which the services are operating but were actively encouraging a precipitate rundown of the mental hospitals as a matter of policy; and that closures would be implemented ruthlessly, leaving little or nothing in their place. We welcome this opportunity to stress that our aim is not the closure or rundown of the mental illness hospitals as such; but rather to replace them with a local and better range of facilities. It will not normally be possible for a mental hospital to be closed until the full range of facilities described in Chapter 4 has been provided throughout its catchment area and has shown itself capable of providing for newly arising patients a comprehensive service independent of the mental hospital. Moreover, even then it will not be possible to close the hospital until it is no longer required for the long stay patients admitted to its care before the local services came into operation.

It was possible to take the view that this was to postpone closure to the Greek Kalends. The White Paper also included an Appendix on 'The Mental Hospitals in the period of Transition to the New Pattern of Service', which expressed the hope that the period of transition would be seen as 'a challenge in the positive sense' and that local managements would give them a share of available manpower and other resources adequate to meet this challenge.

REMAINING PROBLEMS

In the annual report of the Hospital Advisory Service for the year in which NHS reorganisation took place, the director, by then Dr E. Woodford-Williams, commented that in spite of the damaging effect on staff morale of reorganisation, widespread industrial strife in the NHS, and financial stringency, there had been significantly fewer complaints from ex-patients in psychiatric and geriatric hospitals than before; the most critical comments, she went on to say, had been qualified by recognition that staff shortage was the underlying cause.

None the less, when reorganisation took place there was already a further Committee of Inquiry Report in preparation – on South Ockenden Hospital, Essex, published in May 1974 – and events were taking shape at St Augustine's Hospital, Canterbury, which were to issue in March 1976 in the Inskip Report which, *inter alia*, censured the hospital authorities for their failure to give an earlier report by the Hospital Advisory Service 'the attention it deserved'. Clearly the complex and historically conditioned problems of the long-stay hospitals remained one of the most difficult areas with which the reorganised NHS would have to grapple.

6
Open-ended Commitment – Science, Technology and Medical Care

When our first parents were driven out of Paradise, Adam is believed to have remarked to Eve: 'My dear, we live in an age of transition.'   Dean W. R. Inge

Developments in NHS organisation and finance must be seen against the background of developments in medical science and technology, as was made clear in Chapter 2, and the purpose of this chapter is to describe in more detail some of the more significant changes in medical treatment and diagnosis which took place during the years under review and which had implications over and above the contribution they made to the cure or alleviation of disease in individual patients.

THE INFECTIONS

A therapeutic revolution was already taking place when the National Health Service Act came into effect. The expansion of medicine was under way. The basic weapons in the fight against infections and infectious disease had already been forged. Immunisation against diphtheria and vaccination against smallpox were established procedures, although diphtheria still counted among the five notifiable communicable diseases which together caused annually more than 100 deaths per million of the population under 15. Twenty years later, effective and safe immunisation was available against poliomyelitis, measles, tetanus and tuberculosis, and the mortality figures had fallen dramatically. In the early years of the NHS, tuberculosis not only accounted annually for more than

500 deaths per million population, but also for one in every ten days' absence from work through sickness. Twenty years later only one in every seventy days' absence could be ascribed to this cause, and the death rate had fallen by more than 90 per cent.

As far as tuberculosis was concerned, the victory was attributable to a combination of prevention through immunisation, as well as much improved nutritional and living standards generally, and treatment with chemotherapeutic and antibiotic drugs, the successors of prontosil and penicillin, discovered and in use well before the advent of the NHS. Throughout the period under review advances were being made on both these fronts. Successive waves of new antibiotics were introduced as research workers and the pharmaceutical industry sought drugs that would act more specifically against particular bacteria, that would overcome problems of bacterial resistance that had arisen with earlier drugs, or that could be administered more easily and conveniently. By the early 1970s, vaccination against whooping cough was available, although its value was less certain than in the case of the other diseases mentioned, and influenza vaccine was almost ready for widespread use. Unfortunately, influenza was still capable of killing tens of thousands in a single epidemic, so there was intense pressure on the government and medical authorities to make the vaccine available before it had been fully tested.

The consequences of the success experienced during these years in the attack on infectious disease were wide ranging. Already in 1949 many of the 50,000 hospital beds set aside for the treatment of patients suffering from infectious diseases, including tuberculosis, were empty, and under the NHS these were rapidly redesignated for other types of patient. Twenty years later only 10,000 beds remained designated for infectious diseases. Initially, many beds in fever hospitals were taken over for the treatment of tuberculosis, but when, from 1951 onwards, the introduction of first streptomycin, and then PAS and isoniazid, brought about a marked fall in the numbers of tuberculosis patients requiring hospital treatment, many of these beds were then turned over for the care of the chronic sick. Similarly, a proportion of the doctors who had specialised in tuberculosis, or in infectious diseases, turned to geriatrics, forming the nucleus of what was then a new specialty, or they moved into some other field of medicine. A measure of the extent to which the infectious fevers were no longer seen as a major problem was the decision of the General Nursing Council for England and Wales to close the Register of Fever Nurses in 1967. The resources of money, buildings and manpower released by the decline in the infectious diseases acted as a substantial subsidy to other parts of the NHS which were expanding, notably those concerned with the elderly and the chronically sick.

AN AGEING POPULATION

It was appropriate that this was the direction in which resources should be transferred, for one of the problems posed, or at least exacerbated, by the successes of medicine, was that of an ageing population. This was, as described in Chapter 1, a continuation of a trend that had been apparent since at least the turn of the century, but the halving of the overall death rate among young adults, brought about mainly by the control of the infections, gave the trend an additional impetus and focused attention on the need to look ahead to the 1980s and beyond, to provide for a population in which the proportion of elderly would be higher still. By 1973 patients aged 65 and over occupied 45 per cent of all hospital beds (other than in psychiatric hospitals) in England and Wales. Although they constituted only 13 per cent of the total population, they accounted for 20 per cent of hospital discharges and deaths. While geriatrics had emerged as a fully fledged specialty and most district hospitals had a geriatric department, the general medical and surgical wards also contained a high proportion of elderly patients. Some 35 per cent of surgical beds were occupied by patients over 65, and the proportion was rising, while in general medicine the proportion was 46 per cent. The proportion of occupied beds was higher than the proportion of discharges and deaths because, once admitted to hospital, older people tended to stay longer than their younger counterparts. The largest group of elderly patients in hospitals were those suffering from cerebrovascular disease or the neurological consequences of strokes, followed by those suffering from diseases of the heart and arteries, and then cancer of one form or another.

THE PROBLEM OF CANCER

In an ageing population there are inevitably more people suffering from degenerative disorders and from diseases, such as many cancers, which are commoner in later life. Moreover, between 1948 and 1974 the incidence of cancer of the lung was increasing, independently of the age structure of the population, and patients with cancer were being admitted to hospital relatively more frequently as developments in surgery, radiotherapy and chemotherapy offered hope of cure, remission or relief of symptoms. The search for effective forms of treatment for various cancers continued unabated and there were significant advances in the treatment of some of the less common cancers and in the treatment of childhood leukaemia. Unfortunately, many of the drugs used had distressing side-effects, and radiotherapy or treatment with radioactive isotopes could also be extremely unpleasant. The extensive surgery generally indicated in a case of cancer that was not suitable for other forms of treatment was always daunting for the patient, but if some patients who were enabled to survive a few extra months or years were left wondering if it was worth it, others had cause to be grateful both for the surgical techniques which had been developed, often at such specialist centres for cancer as the Royal Marsden Hospital in London, or the Christie Hospital in Manchester, and for the advances in anaesthesiology and applied physiology which enabled patients to withstand such radical operations. The summing up must be that in spite of such advances, cancer remained in 1974 one of the great unsolved problems.

INTENSIVE CARE

Developments in medical technology led during the 1960s to the establishment in many hospitals of intensive care or intensive therapy units, coronary care units and post-operative recovery units. In such units were brought together patients likely to benefit from the use of sophisticated equipment which it was not economic to duplicate widely throughout the hospital, and from the skills of nurses who were accustomed to using such equipment. In a coronary care unit, for example, a patient's heart function could be electronically monitored on a continuous basis so that immediate life-saving action could be taken in the event of malfunction. In other types of intensive care unit the full range of vital functions might be maintained artificially until such time as the patient recovered or was considered dead.

Patients needing continuous observation and maintenance of vital functions after an accident or operation, patients suffering from severe shock from any cause, patients with respiratory or circulatory failure, and cases of drug overdose, all these were considered to be within the remit of such a unit. Improved medical and surgical techniques certainly improved the chances of those patients who had been involved in accidents who reached hospital alive, but during the 1960s two-thirds of all deaths in young men between 15 and 24 were caused by accidents. At the same time, accidents were causing nearly as much absence from work as had tuberculosis before streptomycin. Two out of three accidental deaths were due to road accidents, and deaths from this cause were increasing until 1967, after which there was a slight fall, possibly associated with the introduction of the breathalyser. Most of these deaths occurred before the patient reached hospital and some might have been prevented had it proved possible to deploy at the site of the accident the skills and equipment available in hospitals. This was an organisational problem, and various attempts were made to tackle it, ranging from the training of ambulancemen in advanced resuscitation techniques, to the setting up of a radio network designed to call to the site of an accident any general practitioner who happened to be nearby in the course of his normal work. However, there was great variation in the quality of accident and emergency services in different areas and in many parts little would be done for the patient until he reached hospital.

The wisdom of admitting patients who had had an attack of ischaemic heart disease at home to a coronary care unit was questioned in 1971, when a randomised controlled trial sponsored by the Department of Health suggested that such patients might do better when treated at home than similar patients treated in hospital in a coronary care unit. The experiment was by no means damning as far as coronary care units were concerned, as obviously some patients could not be treated at home because of unsuitable home conditions, and a possible explanation was that some patients found the coronary care unit, with all its equipment, so frightening that they had a further attack. As it might well be possible to make coronary care units less frightening there remained the possibility that in the long run such costly units might indeed be justified in terms of lives saved.

The possibility of maintaining vital functions by artificial means in a patient who was otherwise to all intents and purposes dead raised practical and ethical problems which led to the attempt, in the early 1970s, to reach an agreed definition of 'brain death' which would be acceptable to all doctors, and would help dispel public uneasiness. These efforts did not bear fruit until more than two years after NHS reorganisation, when the Robson Report on 'brain death' was produced by an expert group under the chairmanship of Professor Gordon Robson. At about the same time the DHSS produced a revised post-mortem consent form in an attempt to try to strike a reasonable balance between the rights of deceased patients and their relatives and the need to act quickly if organs were to be removed from a dead patient for transplantation into a living patient whose own organs were diseased.

RENAL TRANSPLANTATION AND DIALYSIS

Most commonly it was the kidneys that were required. A patient whose kidneys failed had little hope of life before the introduction of the artificial kidney, a machine to which the patient's circulation could be connected and which did the job of filtering out waste products which would normally be done by his kidneys. As far as Great Britain was concerned, this technique only came into routine use in 1963. Initially it was only used in hospitals, but by 1964 a few patients were being dialysed in their own homes, and by 1974 there were about 1,500 artificial kidneys installed in patients' homes. However, dialysis had its drawbacks, and for most patients a kidney transplant would have been the treatment of choice, but in the early 1970s only about 450 transplants were being carried out each year, although had the kidneys been available the figure might well have been nearer 2,000. By 1974 efforts were being made to persuade more people to carry cards indicating their agreement to having their kidneys removed in the event of their sudden death, and to refine dialysis techniques to the point where dialysis patients could enjoy a better quality of life.

MONITORING DRUG HAZARDS

It was significant that the research technique used to compare home and hospital treatment of coronary patients was that of the randomised controlled trial pioneered by Sir Austin Bradford Hill, the doyen of medical statistics, in the very early days of the NHS. This was designed to ensure that when two methods of treatment were compared, the division of patients into two groups was on a random basis, so that differences in the characteristics of the two groups themselves did not affect the outcome of the experiment. It was a method admirably suited to the evaluation of new drugs and was widely used for this purpose as the pharmaceutical companies poured an ever-increasing number of new products on to the market. Many of the advances in treatment in these years stemmed from research carried out by the pharmaceutical companies, rather than in university or hospital laboratories. After the initial discovery of penicillin, all subsequent antibiotics originated in commerical laboratories, as did the majority of tranquillizers, hypotensives, antihistamines, anti-malarial drugs, oral contraceptives and new anaesthetic agents.

Many of these new drugs provided the doctor with extremely potent weapons in the fight against disease, but potent drugs have dangers, and the thalidomide tragedy of 1958–61 led to the setting up in 1963 of the Safety of Drugs Committee to scrutinise new drugs and to monitor adverse reactions to all drugs in use. The effectiveness of these new procedures was demonstrated by the subsequent identification of the hazards associated with certain oral contraceptives; on the other hand many hazards could only be identified retrospectively, after some deaths or adverse reactions had occurred, so there remained an irreducible level of risk in the introduction of new products or indeed in the use of any powerful drug, new or old, and the very large number of products available made it difficult for doctors always to choose the most effective drug for a particular patient or to keep abreast of the latest reported side-effects and contraindications.

THE PHARMACEUTICAL INDUSTRY AND THE NHS

The cost of drugs as a proportion of total NHS spending varied little throughout the first twenty-six years but was none the less a constant source of concern to the Ministry and Department of Health. The department bombarded both hospital doctors and general practitioners with information about the comparative costs of different drugs and with exhortations to prescribe, whenever possible, a non-proprietary preparation rather than a branded formulation of the same drug sold, with certain claims as to its greater effectiveness, at a rather higher price. Such exhortations were countered by the drug firms with massive advertising campaigns and through the efforts of representatives who called personally on doctors to explain their firms' products. Other means of promotion used by the companies included the sponsorship of medical conferences and seminars and of medical journals and magazines. All these costs, in addition to the costs of the very substantial investment in research and development which characterised the industry, were ultimately passed on to the customers – and in Britain that meant overwhelmingly the NHS.

Understandably there was continuing controversy as to whether the industry gave value for money, and on the whole relationship between the pharmaceutical industry and the NHS. After a decade of somewhat unsuccessfully trying to influence the prescribing habits of doctors without actually restricting their right to prescribe any drug they chose, the Ministry of Health in 1958 negotiated with the industry an agreement which related the prices charged the NHS to those which firms were able to command in overseas markets where individual patients or their insurance companies paid the bill. The feeling continued to be expressed in Parliament and elsewhere that the drug companies were making excessive profits at the expense of the NHS, and in 1961 Enoch Powell, as Minister of Health, legalised the import of drugs from countries that did not allow pharmaceutical products to be patented, thus effectively holding a pistol at the industry's head. Imports in breach of UK patents were discontinued in 1965 following a further price agreement between the government and the industry.

In the same year, the Sainsbury Report on the Relationship of the Pharmaceutical Industry and the National Health Service recommended the setting up of a Medicines Commission, which was brought into being by the Medicines Act of 1968. Under the Commission a new Committee on the Safety of Medicines was set up which replaced the original Safety of Drugs Committee. The Sainsbury Report also led to further modifications in the prices agreement between the DHSS and the industry, but in 1971 the department referred to the Monopolies

Commission the case of a firm – Roche Products Ltd, the UK subsidiary of the Swiss Hoffmann–La Roche – which had stayed outside the voluntary price regulation scheme, and which supplied nearly 70 per cent of all the tranquillizers prescribed under the NHS. The Monopolies Commission found against the firm and recommended price cuts of 60 and 75 per cent for two of the firm's main products, Librium and Valium, but Roche launched a series of appeals, chiefly on the ground that the Monopolies Commission had not taken into account the high research costs involved in developing such products, and although they were required to reduce their prices legal proceedings were still continuing when NHS reorganisation took place.

PRESYMPTOMATIC SCREENING

The introduction of automated laboratory equipment, such as the multi-channel autoanalyser, made it possible for doctors to think in terms of routinely screening all patients, or at least all patients in certain categories, for a wide range of biochemical abnormalities, and during the 1960s a widespread debate developed on the use of a variety of screening techniques for the detection of latent or presymptomatic disease.

In principle, screening is by no means dependent on advanced technology. The routine examination of schoolchildren for physical defects of one kind or another, practised since the early years of the century, was a form of screening. Mass miniature radiography was outstandingly successful in its day in detecting early cases of pulmonary tuberculosis and enabling them to be treated at a stage when treatment could still offer a good prospect of cure, but the decline in the incidence of tuberculosis meant that latterly the number of cases detected hardly justified either the cost of the service or the radiation risk involved, and in the early 1970s the Department of Health decided to run the service down. Meanwhile, however, a number of other screening techniques had emerged and were being enthusiastically promoted. In some cases it was believed screening would enable treatment to be offered to patients who either were not aware that they were ill, or who for one reason or another had not sought treatment. In other cases it was hoped that early changes in the body or the body fluids would indicate the likelihood of disease developing at a later stage and enable preventive measures to be taken.

Early enthusiasm was replaced towards the end of the 1960s by a more discriminating attitude. It was realised that the detection of physical or biochemical abnormalities in an otherwise healthy individual was not necessarily justification for regarding him as suffering from a disease and in need of treatment. Experience of screening cast doubt on the validity of traditional medical views on the boundary between normal and abnormal, healthy and diseased. Furthermore, it was soon acknowledged that there was little point in screening for diseases which could not, in the existing state of medical knowledge, be treated effectively, or when the treatment facilities available were only barely adequate to cope with the cases that came to light in any case.

A successful use of screening techniques was the routine testing of babies' urine within a few days of birth to detect phenylketonuria, a biochemical defect likely to lead, if untreated, to mental retardation. This was introduced on a large scale in the 1950s and some years later it was estimated that the cost of maintaining the scheme was rather more than justified by the fact that if it had been abandoned about 100 additional children a year would have become mentally retarded. On the other hand, screening for cancer of the neck of the uterus by means of cervical smears taken from women in the age groups considered to be at risk was introduced against a background of pressure from women's organisations and the public generally, even though its value was controversial, and some years after its introduction there was little if any evidence that it was justifying its cost in terms of lives saved. Quite apart from their cost in financial terms, some methods of screening, such as those involving X-ray examination, were not without hazards to the persons screened which had to be balanced against any possible benefits from the detection of disease or abnormality.

THE COMPUTER IN MEDICINE

The electronic computer is potentially useful wherever large masses of data have to be manipulated. Thus by 1974 computers were playing a vital role in the financial management of the NHS. Specifically medical applications were numerous and varied, but many of these were still in the experimental stage. Established applications included the use of computers in medical laboratories to control large numbers of routine tests and process the data derived from them, the use of computers to plan radiotherapy treatment programmes for patients with cancer, and the use of computers in the administration of immunisation programmes. Computers were extensively used in medical research, particularly to process batches of data. The use of computers 'on-line' to store patients' medical records for display at the bedside when required had been explored experimentally, but as far as Great Britain was concerned it seemed likely that it would be a number of years before such applications became widespread.

CENTRAL STERILE SUPPLY AND DISPOSABLES

In the 1950s it became apparent that the system of boiling instruments and syringes in wards, operating theatres and elsewhere in order to sterilise them was unsound and uneconomic. In 1956 the inefficiency of most existing steam autoclaves, which were used for sterilising dressings and other textiles, was demonstrated, and in 1958 a report by the Nuffield Provincial Hospitals Trust gave further publicity to low standards of so-called sterilisation. In the early 1960s new and more efficient steam sterilisers were introduced, but these complex machines needed skilled operators and maintenance, and both their high initial cost and their ability to get through a greater volume of work reinforced the case for centralising sterilising facilities wherever possible.

Some of the early work on the new high-vacuum autoclaves was done at Musgrave Park Hospital, Belfast, which became in 1958 the first NHS hospital to open a central sterile supply department designed to take advantage of the new methods and make sterilisers in wards redundant. At about the same time, there appeared on the market a number of products, such as new types of plastic syringes, which were claimed to be cheap enough to throw away after a single use, thus avoiding the need for resterilisation. There was thus throughout the 1960s lively discussion on such issues as the ideal size, scope and organisation of a central sterile supply department – whether at hospital, group or sub-regional level – and the right balance between the use of disposables, normally supplied by industry, and the use of more durable items which could be resterilised. The new systems relieved nurses of a certain amount of drudgery and thus helped to create time in which they could cope with the faster throughput of patients which was then becoming common. They helped to minimise risks of hospital-acquired infection, although such infection still gave rise to concern. Some doctors and nurses were prepared to argue that the availability of antibiotics to deal with infection when it arose had caused staff to relax their techniques, and to consider it a less serious matter if a wound became infected. With increasing frequency the organisms which gave rise to hospital-acquired infection were found to be resistant to the common antibiotics, and newer, usually more costly, variants had to be invoked. Concern with this problem gave rise to the setting up of infection control committees in most hospitals, and in many to the appointment of an infection control sister to help the bacteriologist monitor the incidence of infection and keep ward techniques under review.

TECHNOLOGICAL ADVANCE AND GENERAL PRACTICE

The availability of so many new and more potent drugs revolutionised general practice no less than hospital medicine. The general practitioner was able to offer effective treatment to many patients whom he would previously have been obliged to refer. By 1974 most general practitioners had direct access to hospital laboratories and diagnostic departments so that they could order investigations themselves rather than have to refer a patient requiring investigation to a consultant merely so that he could sign the form. With more powerful therapeutic and diagnostic weapons in the hands of the general practitioner, it might be thought that hospital outpatient attendances, if not inpatient admissions, would fall. This did not happen, mainly because an ageing population required more hospital treatment, there was a substantial increase in trauma, and the burden of maternity work was shifting to the hospital. Moreover, it is likely that the increase of one-third over twenty years in attendances at hospital casualty departments reflected at least in part the fact that general practitioners had become less accessible. They worked fewer hours, often using deputising services to cover their off duty, they operated appointment systems that did not encourage the casual caller, and in big cities many of them lived some distance from their lock-up surgeries.

Group general practice had already begun in a limited way in the early years of the NHS, but in 1954 new ground was broken in Oxford and Winchester by the experimental attachment of a health visitor to a group general practice. Previously, health visitors had normally covered a defined geographical area rather than the patients of a particular practice, but these experiments were so successful that they marked the start of a widespread movement to attach health visitors and domiciliary nurses and midwives to general practitioners, and the concept of the primary care team, later sometimes extended to include a social worker, grew up. By 1973 only one general practitioner in six was working single-handed and about 75 per cent of health visitors and general practitioners were working together in this type of partnership.

SPECIALISATION IN MEDICINE

Group general practice was only to a limited extent a response to scientific and technological developments, although it did make it possible for some general practitioners to develop their special interests, but in hospital medicine teamwork became essential in the treatment of many patients in order that the full resources of modern medicine and science could be brought to bear. An extreme case would be to consider the number of specialists and technicians likely to be present in the operating theatre during a heart transplant operation in the 1970s compared with the two surgeons, anaesthetist, and three or four nurses who were considered sufficient to embark on the most major operations carried out in 1948. The explosion of medical knowledge and technology was reflected in increasing specialisation within medicine. In 1948 general medicine and surgery were the largest specialities, but while the number of consultants as a whole trebled between 1950 and 1970 (this represented more than a three-fold increase in whole-time equivalents, since a higher proportion of consultants were full-time at the latter date), general medicine and surgery hardly grew at all. The increase was chiefly in specialities newly established, or specialities that were in their infancy when the NHS was inaugurated.

Neurosurgery, thoracic surgery and plastic surgery were recognised as separate specialities in a few centres before 1948, but the NHS established specialist centres in every region. Regional radiotherapy services were also established. Anaesthesiology grew into the largest speciality, followed by pathology and psychiatry, but pathology subdivided and child psychiatry became a specialty in its own right. Geriatrics developed from almost nothing and urology and cardiology separated from general surgery and medicine. There were twice as many recognised specialties in 1973 as in 1949 and there were no signs that the process of increasing specialisation was at an end.

POSTGRADUATE MEDICAL EDUCATION

Accelerating developments in medicine and increasing specialisation created a demand among doctors for more effective means of keeping up to date than reading medical journals and talking to pharmaceutical representatives, and in 1961 doctors in Exeter and Stoke on Trent simultaneously sought to establish local centres of postgraduate medical education. They approached hospital authorities for permission to build on hospital land, and undertook to collect funds themselves for the building, its furnishings and the library. From an early stage the Nuffield Provincial Hospitals Trust took an active interest and eventually provided enough money to help in the setting up of a large number of such centres in various regions.

In 1964 official funds were also made available, and by 1973 there was a postgraduate medical centre in most districts, and a central Council for Postgraduate Medical Education co-ordinated the work of regional postgraduate deans and local tutors. The centres were shared by general practitioners and hospital staff – itself a valuable feature in fostering understanding and communication – and contributed both to the post-registration training of young doctors and to keeping experienced doctors in touch with new developments in their own and other fields. Towards the end of the period it became increasingly common for centres to be concerned with the provision of library facilities and training for other health professions as well as doctors.

PROBLEMS OF SCIENTIFIC ADVANCE

Advances in medical technology clearly brought great benefits to the population served by the NHS, but they also helped to create some of the problems that confronted the service at the time of its reorganisation in 1974. To an even greater extent than when Ffrangcon Roberts made the point in 1952, the relatively easy problems had been solved, and the more difficult ones remained. The increasing use of technology in medicine gave rise to fears that medicine was being dehumanised, that undue reliance upon the machine was causing the doctor's clinical skills to atrophy, and that he was becoming a 'medical machine-minder'. Yet on the other hand studies of general practice showed that a high proportion of patients consulted the doctor for problems that were psychological or psychosomatic in nature rather than purely physical, and although doctors were sometimes accused of prescribing drugs too readily when what was required was an understanding response and a listening ear, there was increasing demand within the profession for the kind of basic medical education and postgraduate training that would enable doctors to deal skilfully with such problems.

In all branches of the profession – except perhaps the surgery of trauma – it was recognised that multiple pathology and chronic disease was the pattern of the 1970s, rather than the isolated episode of acute illness, likely to be shortly resolved one way or the other, which dominated an earlier era of medicine. The doctor's task was frequently not to cure the patient's illness, for more often than not it was too late for that, but to help him come to terms with it and to help him stay as fit as possible in functional terms. Within the field of prevention, the emphasis had shifted from the control of the environment to a need to change patterns of consumption and behaviour believed to be inimical to health, a far more difficult task. Thus, while the 'medical machine-minder' was perhaps one side of the coin at the time of NHS reorganisation, the other was the doctor, in whatever speciality, who found himself obliged as never before – rose-tinted views of the 'good old days' of medicine notwithstanding – to consider his patients as thinking, feeling, individual members of their families, and of society, and as the victims, not so much of the impersonal onslaught of bacteria, as of their own lifestyles and patterns of indulgence.

7
Who Manages the Health Service?

I have heard of hotels that run themselves. If they do, you may be sure that they obey the laws of gravity and run downwards.
Felix Babylon in Arnold Bennett, *The Grand Babylon Hotel*

The administrative structure of the National Health Service, and the roles of the various authorities, have been outlined in Chapter 2. In this chapter we shall subject to closer examination the work of these authorities and the changing pattern of administration and management in the various parts of the service. The discussion will inevitably be dominated by the hospital service, because in terms of both money and manpower it was far bigger than the other two parts of the NHS, and also because during the period under review the pattern of management developed more dynamically in the hospital service than under the executive councils or local health authorities. The family practitioner services were run in very much the same way in 1973 as in the years immediately after 1948 – the greatest change stemmed from the increased popularity of group practices and health centres at the latter end of the period – while changes in local authority services reflected both developments in local government generally and such internal developments as the greater autonomy achieved by local authority nursing services after the publication of the Mayston Report.

The hospital service, however, calls for detailed exploration of such topics as the role and responsibilities of administrators *vis-à-vis* professional, and particularly medical, staff; the participation of senior medical staff in administration; the shifting balance between the individual hospitals and the group, with the eventual emergence of various patterns of 'functional' management; new patterns of administration in the nursing service; the drive towards efficiency and the setting up of extensive programmes to train NHS officers in the theory and techniques of management as practised in industry and in other parts of the public service; the trend towards larger units of organisation; the growth of specialisation in administration etc.

HOSPITAL ADMINISTRATION BEFORE 1948

In so vast an undertaking as the NHS, generalisation is hazardous because however strong the central pressures towards uniformity, local diversity of interpretation and implementation is in the nature of things inevitable, especially when the service is as fragmented as was the NHS in the early years, with no fewer than 388 hospital management committees and 36 boards of governors in England and Wales and a further 84 boards of management in Scotland (compared with the 98 area health authorities in England and Wales and 15 health boards in Scotland in the post-1974 reorganised NHS). It is even more difficult to generalise about patterns of administration in the health service of the pre-1948 era. Apart, however, from local and particular differences and peculiarities, the broad pattern varied between Scotland, and England and Wales; between voluntary and local authority hospitals; within the local authority sector between general hospitals and hospitals for the mentally ill and handicapped; and within the voluntary sector there was a wide range of practice and tradition between the great teaching hospitals and the many small hospitals which made up the bulk of the voluntary sector.

Voluntary hospitals

Typically, in the larger voluntary hospital the chief administrator, or house governor as he was often called, was a man of standing and real power to whom the governors looked for smooth and efficient day-to-day administration, and who enjoyed the confidence and respect of the medical staff. Frequently he also played an important part in fund raising, and his salary was in some cases supplemented by a percentage commission on the money raised. The matron, as head of the nursing service, enjoyed autonomy in her own department and frequently also superintended domestic, linen and perhaps laundry and catering services. These were the two chief officers, there would seldom be a medical superintendent, and only occasionally a treasurer who enjoyed chief officer status.

Local authority hospitals

A local authority hospital, on the other hand, would normally have a medical superintendent who was frequently in clinical as well as administrative charge of the entire hospital, with the steward (administrator) and the matron clearly subordinate to him. The medical superintendent would be answerable to the medical officer of health, who in turn answered to the health committee of the council. The medical officer of health would also be responsible for the local authority nursing, midwifery and health visiting services and if he did not administer them himself they would most likely be administered on his behalf by subordinate medical officers, to whom the senior nurses and midwives would be answerable. In the mental hospitals the pattern of medical superintendency was most firmly established and persisted longest after 1948. Nearly all mental hospitals were divided into male and female sides, headed as far as the nursing was concerned by a chief male nurse and matron respectively, staffed entirely by nurses of the same sex as the patients, and run almost as separate hospitals. The status of the matron and chief male nurse was immeasurably lower than that of the matron in a general, and particularly a voluntary, hospital, and some of the older male chiefs could remember the day when they, or their predecessors, had borne the title 'chief attendant'. The steward, again, was a subordinate officer held in low regard by administrators brought up in the voluntary tradition.

To all these generalisations there were exceptions, and the London County Council, because of the scale of its operation and the way in which it led the field as far as municipal health services were concerned, was a case on its own.

EARLY YEARS OF THE NHS

In the early years of the NHS, the Ministry of Health left HMCs considerable freedom to devise administrative structures suitable to their own circumstances. In groups consisting of more than one hospital the ministry envisaged that there might, at group level, be three senior officers: a secretary, who might also administer one or more of the hospitals in the group; a finance officer; and a supplies officer. It was left to each HMC to decide whether it was necessary to make all three appointments, or whether the responsibilities could be combined in any way. A survey carried out by the Acton Society Trust in 1954 showed that in the 270 non-mental groups, 71 group secretaries combined the responsibilities of that post with other responsibilities (15 with finance, 37 with supplies, 19 with both). There were 217 finance officers and 136 supplies officers, and 6 officers combined finance and supplies. Of the 162 deputy secretaries appointed, 12 also carried responsibility for finance or supplies. In the 118 mental groups, there were only 25 group secretaries who did not also carry responsibility for finance or supplies or both. In Scotland it was, and for many years remained, the universal practice for the chief officer to bear the title 'secretary and treasurer' and to combine these two functions. There were also very few specialist supplies officers in the early years. It was also the practice in Scotland to appoint a group medical superintendent, reflecting the Scottish tradition of administration by medical officers in both voluntary and municipal hospitals.

Group and hospital administration

The relationship between the group administrative staff and the individual hospitals varied from place to place. In the single-hospital group (nearly always a mental group), the group secretary invariably acted also as the hospital secretary. Where he was the former clerk and steward, accustomed to being answerable to the medical superintendent, he found himself in a Pooh Bah situation – as hospital secretary he continued to be answerable to the medical superintendent; as group secretary he represented the HMC to whom the medical superintendent was himself answerable. In multi-hospital groups where the group secretary acted also as hospital secretary of one – usually the principal – of the constituent hospitals, it was sometimes argued that that hospital stood at an advantage in relation to the HMC and to consideration of its needs compared with other hospitals in the group. It was also argued that when the group secretary did not formally act as administrator of the largest hospital, but based his office there, the administrator of the hospital none the less had his authority diminished by the easy accessibility of the chief officer of the HMC.

It was certainly the ministry's intention from the beginning that the group secretary should be seen as a hospital administrator of real authority and standing and not merely as a committee clerk, and so HMCs were exhorted to appoint men and (most exceptionally) women with experience of hospital administration. On the other hand, many senior administrators were themselves convinced that the group secretary would in effect be little more than a committee clerk, able to exercise but slender influence over the way in which individual hospital secretaries ran their hospitals. Hospitals, this line of thinking ran, were the places where patients were cared for, where the influential medical staff felt their loyalties lay, they were the true power base. Few senior administrators carried this line of thinking far enough to refuse to compete for group secretary posts, but it was some consolation to those who were unsuccessful, and was indeed the source of tension between 'group' and the individual hospitals which was a feature of the hospital service in many areas throughout much of the period.

The medical superintendent

The position of the medical superintendent as administrative head of a mental hospital was specifically protected under the NHS, although the relationship of his responsibilities under certain statutes for evey patient in his hospital with the clinical responsibilities of other consultants working in the hospital was somewhat ambiguous. In other former local authority hospitals run by medical superintendents there was, however, a change. The responsibilities of the medical superintendent were drastically reduced, some being transferred to the hospital secretary, and individual holders of the post were mostly given the choice of competing for consultant appointments, with purely clinical responsibilities, or retaining the title of medical superintendent and some of the functions at a salary rather less than that of a consultant. Some medical superintendents who did not have the qualifications for a consultant appointment were graded as senior hospital medical officers (SHMOs).

The matron

When the NHS came into being the position of the matron in many hospitals was already changing. Increasingly in the years before 1948, hospitals, both voluntary and municipal, had been appointing laundry, linen, domestic and catering superintendents and making them responsible to the administrator, rather than to the matron, who was divested of these responsibilities and in many hospitals became purely and simply head of the nursing service. The NHS accelerated this trend, even though in small isolated hospitals matrons continued to function also as housekeepers for many years to come. Not all matrons were pleased to be relieved of their other responsibilities and the NHS was blamed for what was seen as a loss of status. Further loss of status was felt by those matrons who had been accustomed to attending meetings of their board of governors, or committee, but who were not invited to attend meetings of the HMC. In a group of twenty hospitals it was clearly impractical for all matrons to attend; some HMCs instituted a system whereby one matron represented her colleagues, but without any authority over them and without implying any such thing as the appointment of a 'group matron'. Other HMCs left the communication of policy and the forwarding of nursing views to the group secretary, and this was much resented.

THE GUILLEBAUD AND BRADBEER REPORTS

The pattern of administration in hospitals and hospital groups came under early review, to some extent in the report of the Guillebaud Committee on the Cost of the NHS and in considerable detail in the

1954 Bradbeer Report on the Internal Administration of Hospitals. The Bradbeer Committee held that hospital administration was a tripartite affair, subdivided into medical administration, nursing administration, and lay, or business, administration. The boundaries between the three parts could not be sharply defined, even in theory, let alone in practice, so what was called for was a concept of partnership that allowed for a great deal of flexibility and accommodation to both circumstances and the personal characteristics and capacities of individual officers. To recommend any one rigid pattern of organisation would be, the Committee felt, fatal. For this reason many recommendations were expressed tentatively or hedged about with qualifications, but on one point the Committee were firm. At group, as distinct from hospital, level, there must be one chief administrative officer to whom the Committee could look to see that policies were carried out and to co-ordinate and review all group activities. Except in groups consisting of a single mental hospital, this chief administrative officer would be a layman, the group secretary. The Bradbeer Committee felt there was no place for group matrons or group medical superintendents, but they were in favour of the group secretary's also acting as the administrator of the largest hospital in the group. If he did not also administer a hospital there was a danger that he would loose the 'feel' of hospital life and get out of touch with the practical problems of hospital administration.

The difficulties that were later to be experienced by unit hospital administrators with the emergence of 'functional' patterns of administration were already present in embryo in 1954. The Bradbeer Committee referred to the arguments put forward by finance officers that while finance staff working within a hospital must be under the control and subject to the discipline of the administrator of that hospital, as far as their financial work was concerned they should be accountable to the group finance officer and work to his instructions. The Committee, however, accepted the view put forward by the King's Fund and the Institute of Hospital Administrators that specialist staff working within a hospital should be accountable to the hospital administrator. On balance they preferred 'to see the unit hospital administrator paramount in the lay administration of his own hospital'. None the less this was the beginning, rather than the end, of this particular controversy, and over the next twenty years hospital secretaries steadily lost ground to the functional specialists, and the post of hospital secretary diminished in status to such an extent that towards the end of the period under review it became generally a post held for a short time by a young administrator on his way up, or a backwater into which were shunted the older administrators who were not considered to have the potential for further promotion.

The Bradbeer Committee also reviewed the question of house committees, which had been created in many groups to reflect the continued identity of individual hospitals, but which the ministry did not believe should be given executive powers lest an extra tier of administration be created. The Report agreed that these non-statutory committees should not be given authority to spend Exchequer money, but felt they did useful work, especially in relation to patient welfare and links with the local community. The Guillebaud Report endorsed this view.

The Bradbeer and Guillebaud Committees both discussed the composition of the hospital authorities themselves. On average, 20–30 per cent of HMC and RHB members were doctors, and at times the proportion was as high as 40 per cent, although mental HMCs tended to have fewer, perhaps 5–15 per cent, doctor members. Other professional groups in the health service were rarely represented (the doctors were not, of course, strictly representatives of their colleagues, but were appointed as individuals, or in some cases as representatives of a university). Arguments had been put forward that membership of hospital authorities should also be open to other groups of staff, but the Bradbeer Committee felt that doctors were a special case, and it would be particularly objectionable for an administrator to be a member of his own authority – in which case he would be participating in the making of policies it was his duty to implement – or of another authority, in which case he might be subject to divided loyalties. The Guillebaud Committee, whilst agreeing that doctors were a special case, thought that generally medical members should not exceed 25 per cent on any board or committee.

THE FARQUHARSON-LANG REPORT

These two Reports did not look in detail at the actual work which boards and committees did and the matters with which they concerned themselves. This was, however, part of the brief given to the Farquharson-Lang Committee, set up in 1962 by the Scottish Health Services Council, and when the Committee's Report on Administrative Practices of Hospital Boards in Scotland appeared in 1966 it was generally agreed that much of what they had to say was true also of England and Wales. Indeed, certain passages in the Report were subsequently commended to the attention of hospital authorities in England and Wales by the Ministry of Health – although these did not include the recommendation that each hospital group should have a chief executive, a suggestion that was quickly seen to have fallen on fallow ground even in Scotland.

The Farquharson-Lang Report painted a picture of the activities of some hospital boards which was quickly recognised as having wide validity throughout the NHS. Hospital authorities were concerning themselves over much with detail at the expense of broad policy. There was a proliferation of sub-committees, and meetings went on for hours discussing matters that ought to have been decided by officers who were paid, and who increasingly were trained, as responsible managers able to take such decisions. House committees in particular were prone to deal with trivia. (It was possible to suspect that in some instances officers took trivial matters to committee not because they could not take the decisions themselves, but in order to give the committee something to do, or even, perhaps, to distract them from other more important matters which the officers did not wish to have discussed by members who lacked the detailed and expert knowledge that they themselves possessed.) One or two examples drawn from the Farquharson-Lang Report indicate the level of the matters referred to.

Various requests for junior staff for leave of absence to sit examinations were granted.

The Committee selected a suitable colour for the cards to be attached to food carriers at . . . hospital.

It was resolved that certain glass windows should be replaced and meshed after breakage by truant boys.

The Committee were shown a counterpane which had shrunk to half its proper size.

It was resolved to investigate the matter.

'JUMBO' GROUPS AND FUNCTIONAL MANAGEMENT

The Farquharson-Lang Report had a salutary effect on the tendency to proliferate sub-committees and persuaded many authorities to delegate more business to officers. A trend which assisted this development was the number of amalgamations which took place during the late 1950s and the 1960s and which led to the creation of larger, and in some cases very large, hospital groups in which it would not have been possible for the committee to deal with every detail, especially when shorn, under prompting from the ministry, of most of their sub-committees. The Birmingham Region led the way in the creation of these 'jumbo' groups of perhaps 3,000 or more beds, and after the 1959 Mental Health Act, with its emphasis on the integration of treatment facilities for the mentally disordered with other branches of medicine, the one-hospital mental group rapidly became exceptional, the big mental hospital usually being taken into a neighbouring general group and the HMC being reconstituted accordingly.

The 'jumbo' groups led the way in a trend towards functional patterns of management based on the view that the hospital group was the basic entity and that administrative organisation should reflect the services which administration provided rather than the identity of individual hospitals within the group. Thus hospital secretaries – or unit administrators as they came to be called – found they were being increasingly bypassed by lines of command flowing from specialists (e.g. caterers, domestic managers, engineers, building supervisors, personnel officers) working within the hospital to their counterparts at group headquarters. A few groups attempted to do without the post of unit administrator, but in most patterns of so-called functional management geographical and functional spheres of authority overlapped and were at times in conflict. The trend towards functional management reflected both an increasing concern with efficiency and a desire on the part of each occupational group to increase the number and standing of the top jobs available to its members. A typical progression was for posts at hospital level to be upgraded from supervisory to managerial, followed by the establishment of a group post to co-ordinate the managers in the individual hospitals and to develop the service in the group as a whole. This would most likely be followed by a call for the establishment of an advisory post at region, and perhaps by the suggestion that the group service manager should be made answerable directly to the HMC rather than to the administrator. This last move was successful to some extent with the hospital engineers, but for the most part the administrators were able to hold the line at this point. A number of specialist groups, however, found themselves well poised by 1973 to advance their status still further in the reorganised health service with a claim for the establishment of posts at district and area levels.

RECRUITMENT AND TRAINING OF HOSPITAL ADMINISTRATORS

Meanwhile, other developments had ensued from the anxiety expressed by the Guillebaud Committee about existing arrangements for the recruitment and training of hospital administrators. Some of the evidence received by the Committee suggested authorities were having difficulty in making suitable appointments to senior posts, and there was no national scheme of training designed to ensure a future supply of able administrators. Some authorities had their own schemes, or participated in joint schemes, and King Edward's Hospital Fund for London set up in 1951 the Hospital Administrative Staff College, which organised courses for both senior and junior staff and acted as a centre for research and study into problems of hospital administration. That, however, is all there was.

The Guillebaud Committee urged that a national scheme for the recruitment and training of hospital administrators should be developed and that steps should be taken to ensure a suitable career structure. In any such structure, the Committee felt, the post of hospital secretary should be seen as one of key importance. If the position and status of the hospital secretary had been impaired in the course of building up the 'group idea', then this was regrettable, and provision should be made to ensure that in terms of salary, prospects and responsibilities the post of hospital secretary would be attractive to able administrators.

The Noel Hall Report

As a result of what Guillebaud had to say on this topic, the Ministry of Health set up in collaboration with the Hospital Administrative Staff College and the University of Manchester a national training scheme for a small number of young graduates and other young people of promise already in the service, and then in 1957 invited Sir Noel Hall, principal of the Administrative Staff College at Henley, to undertake a personal inquiry into the grading and salary structure of administrative and clerical staff. The basic problem with which Sir Noel had to grapple was that of providing a satisfactory career structure in a service made up of nearly 400 employing authorities, each entitled to appoint officers of their own choosing to posts at all levels. The grading structure and salary scales were centrally controlled and subject to negotiation on the Administrative and Clerical Staffs Whitley Council, but there was no way of providing an officer faced with a promotion bottleneck in his own authority with an opening in the service of another authority; no way of ensuring uniform standards in the selection of recruits to the service; no way of arranging for an officer to have in the course of his career varied experience of different types of work and hospital authority, other than by encouraging him to apply, in competition with others, for posts as they fell vacant.

In addition, the Whitley Council grading structure was thought by many to be unduly rigid, with too many fine distinctions leading to overspecialisation in the lower and middle grades and to difficulties in giving officers the opportunity to widen their experience even within the same employing authority. It was also argued that the career prospects in hospital administration were insufficiently attractive to draw into the service a fair share of the brighter school-leavers, and that the age structure of the service was in danger of becoming unbalanced, with a disproportionate number of senior officers in the higher age groups.

Sir Noel examined a number of the more sweeping suggestions which had been made and rejected, for instance, the idea of a national appointing authority to appoint officers to posts anywhere in the country. Like the Bradbeer and Guillebaud Committees, he stressed the need to preserve the autonomy of the individual hospital authority, and he placed similar emphasis on the role of the hospital secretary. None the less his report foreshadowed in many ways the more centralising recommendations of the Lycett Green Committee a few years later. Hospital authorities should retain in their own hands the power of appointment of senior officers, but representatives of RHBs should participate in the appointment of senior officers by HMCs. He recommended a simplified and uniform system of grading, and a scheme based on his recommendations was introduced in 1958. His report also resulted in the setting up in each region of a staff advisory committee to advise employing authorities and individual officers on career prospects, vacancies, and similar matters, and to organise and supervise training schemes for administrative staff. A system of outside assessors to sit on appointments committees was introduced.

As a result of the new emphasis on training, some regions appointed regional training officers and in 1961 others were urged by the ministry to follow suit. In 1962 the national training scheme for hospital administrators was supplemented by a scheme devised to have a more practical emphasis and to be run by the regions, rather than nationally, the two schemes for the time being to run in parallel. A shortage of potential finance officers had been noted, so this scheme included special provision for candidates wishing to specialise in finance. In the same year the Lycett Green Committee were set up to inquire into the recruitment, training and promotion of administrative and clerical staff in the hospital service, and their Report was published in 1963.

The Lycett Green Report
The Lycett Green Report recommended that a National Staff Committee should be set up to oversee the recruitment and training of hospital administrators and to advise on appointments and promotions procedures. There should be regional staff committees to implement the policies of the National Staff Committee. The existing national and regional schemes of training should be merged in a single scheme of two years' duration (instead of two-and-a-half). The general pattern of training should be prescribed by the National Staff Committee. Within this pattern, regional staff committees should plan the practical training and the training institutions (i.e. the Hospital Administrative Staff College and the Universities of Manchester and Leeds) should plan the course of theoretical study; they should collaborate closely to ensure the integration of theory and practice. A system of planned movement should be introduced to enable hospital administrators who had com-

pleted their basic training to gain varied experience in different types of work and under different hospital authorities, and a system of annual staff reports, based on that used in the Civil Service, should be brought in for all former trainees and for those officers who, whilst they had not been through a formal training scheme, wished to be considered for advancement. Management courses of three months' duration should be organised for senior officers and steps should be taken toward the standardisation of appointments procedures and criteria. Recommendations were also made to improve and rationalise the recruitment of clerical staff to the hospital service.

Most of the Lycett Green recommendations were accepted by the Ministry of Health and subsequently implemented. A National Staff Committee was set up, with a regional staff committee in each region. The reorganised training scheme recruited a steady flow of able young graduates to the hospital service and enabled some non-graduates already in the service to experience a modicum of formal training. The practical attachments were not always successful in providing useful opportunities for learning or in stretching the abilities of the trainees, but this depended very much on the capacity and interest of preceptors on the spot. The theoretical component of the course was steadily whittled down and once this was reduced to less than twelve months the University of Manchester trainees lost the advantage they had formerly enjoyed, of being eligible for the award of a university Diploma in Social Administration. Some of the changes in the scheme were clearly the result of pressures from administrators who feared the emergence of an élite group who would expect accelerated promotion and affect adversely the careers of the humble plodders in the service. Apart from the Manchester DSA, no other formal qualification was ever associated with the scheme and it did not profess to prepare trainees for what was regarded as the normal professional qualification for administrators, the Diploma of the Institute of Hospital Administrators. At times there was concern (seldom openly expressed) at the proportion of women recruited to the scheme. This reflected the abilities of those who applied for training rather than any deliberate policy, but relatively few women trainees subsequently pursued careers in line management; such specialist functions as personnel, training and planning providing havens for many of them. (When the NHS came to be reorganised, only one woman was to be found among the ninety-eight newly appointed area administrators in England and Wales.) The system of planned movement was never a great success, nor did the staff reporting system fulfil early hopes. In many hospital groups it quickly became one more piece of paperwork to be completed rather than an opportunity to guide and counsel a subordinate.

THE MANAGEMENT OF HOSPITAL NURSING SERVICES

Meanwhile, both nurses and doctors had been having thoughts about their contribution to the overall management of the NHS. In spite of the opposition of the Bradbeer Committee to the appointment of a 'group matron', it was increasingly felt by nursing administrators that by continuing to emphasise the hospital rather than the group as the basic unit of organisation they were missing the opportunity to influence the policies and decisions of the hospital authorities. A few group matrons were appointed during the 1950s, and the male and female sides of a number of mental hospitals were unified under one nursing manager, usually bearing the title of 'principal nursing officer'. Otherwise there was little development until 1963, when the Salmon Committee were appointed to advise on the senior nursing staff structure in the hospital service, the administrative functions of the respective grades, and the methods of preparing staff to occupy them. However, an early indication of the way senior members of the profession were thinking was given by the publication in 1964 of a Royal College of Nursing report *Administering the Hospital Nursing Service.*

The Royal College of Nursing suggested – and clearly hoped the Salmon Committee would note the suggestion – that each hospital group should appoint a 'group nursing officer', whose span of control would equate with that of the group secretary, and that each hospital would have a 'hospital nursing officer' whose span of control would equate with that of the hospital secretary. When the Salmon Report was published in 1966 it recommended that the hospital nursing service should in future be organised on the basis of the group, rather than the individual hospital, and that each hospital group of any size would have a chief nursing officer responsible directly to the governing body, although in order that he might perform his co-ordinating function she would report to the group secretary or secretary to the board.

Nurse administrators would be divided into numbered grades according to the level of responsibility carried. Grade 6 would be first-line management, that is the level of management represented by a ward sister or nurse in charge of a department. Grades 7 and 8 would be middle management grades, and the report suggested the titles nursing officer and senior nursing officer respectively. Grade 9 would be a principal nursing officer, typically in charge of a division consisting either of a single large hospital or two or more smaller hospitals. In hospital groups too small to merit a chief nursing officer, grade 10, the top nursing post might be graded 9, but otherwise the principal nursing officers in a group, including the principal nursing officer in charge of the education division, or school of nursing, and the principal nursing officer in charge of midwifery, would be responsible to the chief nursing officer. The fact that a chief nursing officer might not be professionally qualified in every field of nursing for which she was responsible, e.g. as a mental nurse or a midwife, was not felt to matter. She was primarily a manager of nursing services. Clinical expertness in the various fields of nursing was more appropriately located at a lower point in the heirarchy.

There was no place in this structure for assistant and deputy matrons working in the traditional way, as assistants to the matron, carrying out whatever tasks she assigned them, without defined responsibilities of their own. The post of assistant matron in a traditional hospital was notoriously unsatisfying to nurses of real ability. A few hospitals had already broken away from this pattern with the appointment of 'clinical assistant matrons', each responsible to the matron for the nursing management of a group or block of wards and departments, but the Salmon Committee decided that in future this pattern of delegated responsibility should be the norm. The Committee also recommended that nurse administrators should be relieved of the control of services for the management of which nursing knowledge was not required, and that they should be systematically prepared for their responsibilities as managers by attending management courses and by being given training on the job. There should be national and regional staff committees for nurses on the lines of those already established for hospital administrators, and these committees should establish uniform procedures for selecting nurses for senior posts and should oversee the provision of management training for senior nurses.

The Ministry of Health decided to try out the new structure in a few hospital groups, carefully selected to be representative of the different types of group to be found in the country as a whole – teaching and non-teaching; mental, general and mixed; large, middling and small – before endorsing it for general adoption. However, before the pilot schemes had been evaluated, the National Board for Prices and Incomes produced Report No. 60 (see Chapter 3), which urged that the Salmon Report should be implemented immediately, on a nationwide basis, as a means of improving the management of the nursing service. The ministry accepted this recommendation, but over the next year or two it became apparent that there was a serious shortage of candidates of the requisite calibre for the most senior Salmon appointments, and the wisdom of 'instant Salmon' was therefore called in question. On the other hand the original plan would have meant a prolonged period of uncertainty that would not have been good for the morale of the nursing service, and with the traditional and new structures existing side by side over a long period there would have been many anomalies in pay and conditions of service. Moreover the fact that in most parts of the country the new structure was by 1974 well established and hundreds of senior nurses had gained valuable experience of large-scale management meant that the profession was far more ready than it would otherwise have been to play a key part in NHS reorganisation and the setting up of new structures for the NHS as a whole.

A National Nursing Staff Committee for England and Wales was set up in 1967, but regional nursing staff committees were not felt to be necessary. The NNSC shared premises with the National Staff Committee for hospital administrators, and in 1968 Dame Isobel Graham Bryce was appointed chairman of both. The NNSC worked hard to establish standardised procedures, embodying outside assessors, for appointments to senior nursing posts, and to set up a scheme of staff appraisal and counselling. They launched a massive programme of management training for all grades of nurse from ward sister upwards, and if at times this resembled a sheep-dip rather than a truly educational exercise it did wonders for the self-confidence of nurse managers *vis-à-vis* their counterparts in other professions.

THE MANAGEMENT OF LOCAL AUTHORITY NURSING SERVICES

The local authority nursing field had special problems of its own which made it impossible simply to apply the recommendations of the Salmon Report without further consideration. Numbers of staff were smaller, both in total and for the most part in individual authorities when compared with hospital groups. Local authorities were not merely, like HMCs, agents of the secretary of state, but independent corporate bodies with a wide range of statutory functions in addition to health. The medical officer of health or county medical officer had overall responsibility for the health department, including the nursing services; the nursing services had themselves developed in different ways in different areas, with a chief nursing officer co-ordinating all services in some, but with separate superintendents for district nursing, midwifery and health visiting in others.

In 1968, therefore, the Mayston Committee were set up to consider the application of the Salmon principles to local authority nursing services. A year later they recommended that all authorities that had not already done so should appoint a chief nursing officer, to equate with Salmon grade 10, 9 or 8 according to the size of the authority. The chief nursing officer should be responsible to the medical officer of health or county medical officer rather than directly to the health committee, but medical officers should no longer be personally responsible for organising and administering nursing services. Below the chief nursing officer it was felt the local authority nursing service did not require as many grades as the Salmon Report had recommended and it was suggested that first-line managers of community nursing services should equate with Salmon grade 7. The Mayston Committee set out alternative organisational charts, allowing the service to be organised either on the basis of geographical areas, integrating home nurses, health visitors and midwives in one workforce, or on the basis of professional specialism, but they made it clear that they preferred the geographical form of organisation.

THE MANAGEMENT OF HOSPITAL MEDICAL SERVICES

Now the Bradbeer Committee had seen the management of hospitals as a partnership between medical, nursing and lay elements, but as far as the medical element was concerned they felt the medical committee system, both at hospital and group level, needed to be strengthened, and they were not in favour of group medical superintendents. There for the most part the matter rested until 1967, when the first report appeared of a Joint Working Party on the Organisation of Medical Work in Hospitals which had been set up by the Ministry of Health with the Joint Consultants Committee, representing consultant medical staff in the hospital service. Although the working party was chaired by Sir George Godber, chief medical officer of the Ministry of Health, the report quickly became known as the 'Cogwheel Report' because of the device which appeared on the cover. On the same day that the Cogwheel Report appeared, the Scottish Home and Health Department published the Brotherston Report, which represented the deliberations of a Scottish working party on identical terms of reference. The main recommendations of the two reports were on similar lines. Specialties falling into the same broad medical or surgical categories within a hospital or hospital group should be brought together to form divisions, each division should have a chairman – the Scots thought he should be elected, the English suggested he should be appointed by the regional board or board of governors – and representatives of the divisions should come together as a medical executive committee. The Cogwheel Report envisaged that the chairman of the medical executive committee would be a clinician with time in his contract for administrative duties, so that he could serve both as a part-time medical administrator and as chief medical spokesman for the hospital or group of hospitals. Such an administrative role for the chairman was not envisaged by the Scottish working party since most of the duties embraced by it were already discharged in Scottish hospitals by the medical superintendent.

Both reports discussed a number of detailed issues in medical administration but were careful to avoid any suggestion that might seem to curtail the right of each individual consultant to treat his patients as he thought best. The working parties both took the opportunity to disseminate information about a number of innovations in the organisation of hospital medical services which had taken place in various hospitals over the previous few years. These included the pooling of emergency beds to avoid too many beds being kept empty for emergencies while other patients waited for admission, the undertaking of an increasingly wide range of medical investigations on an outpatient basis, the use of five-day wards (avoiding the need to provide staff at weekends), the use of day hospitals, intensive care units and pre-discharge wards. Both reports also spoke of the need for doctors to have management training and of the value of bringing clinicians together with non-medical administrators in joint management courses.

In a circular to hospital authorities the following year the Ministry of Health asked them to encourage their medical staffs to organise themselves along the lines suggested. Progress was slow, however, and by 1973 only about half the hospital groups in England and Wales had set up both clinical divisions and a medical executive committee. Some had set up divisions, but not a medical executive committee, preferring to retain their existing medical advisory committee, consisting often of the entire consultant staff, or those among them who cared to attend a particular meeting. One or two had set up a medical executive, but had not formed divisions. In one or two regions progress had been impeded by the reluctance of the RHB to allocate money to enable the chairman of the medical executive to spend time on administrative duties, and for secretarial help. The Cogwheel Report was never intended to be a detailed blueprint, and there were many local variations in the arrangements made. In some cases the new Cogwheel system superseded existing medical committees, in others it was set up alongside them. At best the new system was of real value in providing a forum where medical opinion could crystallise and an opportunity for the administration to delegate to the doctors certain executive functions which it was not possible to delegate until effective machinery for their discharge existed. A common example was the spending of the financial allocation for medical equipment and deciding on priorities between competing items.

The more sanguine hopes that the setting up of a Cogwheel structure would lead to more rational use of beds, closer co-operation with the administration and with the other professions, the extension of peer group review of clinical results, and a greater consciousness generally among consultants of the need to use strictly limited resources to maximum effect, could hardly be fully realised in the short term. Cogwheel structures needed time to take root and it was unfortunate that re-organisation of the NHS took place before, in most places, this could occur. However, the setback may prove to be only temporary, and indeed by 1974 it was already possible to quote examples of Cogwheel structures that were making an important contribution to the management of the hospital group and realising many of the hopes of the joint working party.

8

The Health Service and Social Change

A nurse and a leading plastic surgeon have been shot dead in Madrid by a man who was dissatisfied with the results of an operation to correct a nose fault.

Nursing Mirror, 24 March 1977

THE RISE OF THE CRITICAL CONSUMER

One facet of social change that had its impact on the National Health Service – the rise of the critical consumer – was predicted by Bevan himself when he looked forward to the much-needed improvements that he believed the National Health Service Act would make possible. The quality of the hospitals which were being taken over varied enormously, and that could not be put right overnight, but the Act would make it possible to secure a more even distribution of consultants, thus raising standards in many places, and the vesting of responsibility in the minister would ensure a new responsiveness to public wishes and complaints.

After 5 July [he said] the Minister of Health will be the whipping-boy for the Health Service in Parliament. Every time a maid kicks over a bucket of slops in a ward an agonized wail will go through Whitehall. After the new Service is introduced there will be a cacophony of complaints. The newspapers will be full of them. I am sure some doctors will make irate speeches. The Order Paper of the House of Commons will be filled with questions. For a while it will appear that everything is going wrong. As a matter of fact, everything will be going right, because people will be able effectively to complain.

They complain now but nobody heeds them. What the Health Act will do after 5 July is to put a megaphone in the mouth of every complainant, so that he will be heard all over the country.

And on another occasion: 'I shall try to go about disguised after 5 July. Any mistake that is made I shall have to bleed for. I shall be going about like Saint Sebastian pierced by a thousand javelins.'

But although after more than a decade another Minister of Health was indeed listening to a 'cacophony of complaints', they were not of the kind Bevan had in mind, not so much from patients and the public, but from those working within the NHS. Enoch Powell, Minister of Health 1960–3, wrote in his book, *A New Look at Medicine and Politics*:

> One of the most striking features of the National Health Service is the continual deafening chorus of complaint which rises day and night from every part of it . . . The universal Exchequer financing of the service endows everyone providing it as well as using it with a vested interest in denigrating it, so that it presents what must be the unique spectacle of an undertaking that is run down by everyone engaged in it.

Complaints against hospitals and doctors were by no means unknown before 1948 – the 1937 PEP Report commented that some voluntary hospitals did not always handle patients' complaints as well as they might, taking refuge behind a general defence that they were engaged in a great philanthropic work and that mistakes inevitably occurred. On the other hand, those who are in receipt of charity seldom feel in a strong position to complain. As far as the public hospitals were concerned, although the PEP Report suggested that the involvement of elected councillors in their management was a safeguard to the public, it is likely that lingering associations with the old Poor Law may have had a similar inhibiting effect. Nor was it to be expected that such inhibitions and attitudes would disappear overnight with the passage of an Act which secured treatment and service for all, as of right, from the national Exchequer, to which all contributed according to their ability to pay. As late as the 1960s and early 1970s successive surveys showed a marked reluctance on the part of patients to complain, even when there was quite evidently something to complain about. More often than not it was workers within the service, rather than patients themselves, or their relatives, who drew attention to conditions and practices which could no longer be regarded as acceptable.

However, despite the passivity of the majority of patients, the 1960s were a period during which the consumer voice began to be heard in the NHS in a way that had not been experienced before. Such publications as Gerda Cohen's outspoken 1964 Penguin Special *What's Wrong with Hospitals?* came as a shock to many doctors and nurses, especially as she attributed many of the failings she described to outdated attitudes on the part of hospital staff. However, they had already been warned by Enoch Powell, speaking as the responsible minister, to beware of the gulf in outlook, sympathy and comprehension that could open up between the inside world of the hospital, so tight, so warm, so perfect, so completely under control, and the outside world populated 'by peculiar, unreasonable, ungrateful creatures – patients and patients' relatives, forsooth, and, who knows, general practitioners, local authorities and councillors, taxpayers, ratepayers, voluntary bodies – even perhaps the odd MP or two'. As minister, Powell had been sharply critical of attitudes in some of the maternity hospitals he had visited at a time when the maternity service in particular was under attack from a new, self-confident generation of young mothers, who wanted to understand more of what was happening to them, who disliked what they felt to be the conveyor-belt atmosphere of some maternity hospitals, and who in some cases wanted their husbands with them during delivery – a practice that obstetricians and midwives were often reluctant to allow.

Such pressures led to the founding of the Association for Improvement in Maternity Services (AIMS). Similarly, the National Association for the Welfare of Children in Hospital was formed in 1961 (originally as 'Mother Care for Children in Hospital') to hammer home the message spelled out in the 1959 Platt Report on the Welfare of Children in Hospital, that children needed regular and continuing contact with their parents. The Association campaigned for the universal adoption of unrestricted visiting in children's wards, for the provision of accommodation to enable mothers to stay in hospital with their children, and for better play facilities in children's wards. At times they met stiff resistance from paediatricians and paediatric ward sisters who felt that frequent visiting was upsetting for the child and were not impressed by evidence which purported to show that separation from the mother could give rise to long-term psychological problems.

The principal generic group were the Patients Association, founded in the early 1960s following a letter to the *Observer* from a woman who alleged she had been subject to medical experimentation during her pregnancy, and over the next few years the subject of medical experimentation and the question of the patient's right to refuse to be used for the teaching of medical students were the chief preoccupations of the Patients Association. Gradually, however, the Association broadened their concerns and took up a wider range of issues. They also did a good deal of casework, helping individuals to pursue complaints and drawing the attention of health authorities to the need to take such complaints seriously. The chief problem such an association faced was shortage of money, for patients are a transient group and it was difficult to accept money from sources other than the membership for fear of being compromised.

A high proportion of complaints seemed to stem from failures of communication or from a lack of consideration of the patient as an individual with feelings and a sense of his own dignity. These themes also emerged from some of the research into patients' perceptions of health care which was being done about this time. Indeed, 'bad communications' became during the 1960s a portmanteau explanation for almost every possible failure of care or management in the health service. It was given academic respectability in the work of R. W. Revans, whose original research embodied in his book *Standards for Morale*, first published in 1964, led him to suggest a close connection between communications, staff morale and turnover, and the rate at which patients recovered in a hospital. In 1961 the Standing Medical and Nursing Advisory Committees of the Central Health Services Council set up a joint sub-committee under the chairmanship of Lord Cohen of Birkenhead to advise how best hospital patients, and their relatives, might be provided with the information they should have on diagnosis, prognosis and treatment. The Report, which came out in 1963, suggested that the best features of good general practice, especially the continuing responsibility of the practitioner for his patient's welfare, set a useful pattern for hospital work, and that this situation could best be replicated in hospital by the designation for each patient of a 'personal doctor' – normally the responsible consultant or his deputy – who would be known personally to the patient, would listen to his problems, explain the nature and purpose of investigations, and reassure him about his treatment and its aftermath. This recommendation was not greeted with enthusiasm by hospital doctors, who tended to feel not only that the report presented an idealised view of general practice, but that hospital patients knew perfectly well whom to ask for information if they wanted it.

On the other hand, some of the surveys of patient opinion commissioned by such bodies as the King Edward's Hospital Fund for London and the Institute of Community Studies, suggested that patients wanted information but were reluctant to ask if they were not given it. More than 60 per cent of patients interviewed for Ann Cartwright's 1964 study, *Human Relations and Hospital Care*, mentioned some failure in communication, although only about half of these failures appeared to give rise to serious dissatisfaction. Other studies confirmed the finding that poor communications were the commonest cause of complaint in hospitals. That at least was how it appeared at the time. It was left to Michael Wilson to point out more than ten years later, in his *Health is for People*, that some instances of supposed 'poor communication' may in fact represent extremely effective, if unconscious, communication of an underlying attitude that, for instance, the important thing about a patient is his clinical condition, or that the doctor's concern is essentially with the patient and his clinical problems, and that the patient's relatives have but a peripheral place in the hospital scheme of things.

Some of Winifred Raphael's research hammered home the point that although staff may feel they are speaking for the patients when they call for better facilities for care and treatment, patients themselves order their priorities rather differently. Staff were likely to put buildings and equipment at the top of the list. Patients tended to feel most strongly about interpersonal relations, attitudes, and, again, communications – as well as such basic, non-medical, amenities as clean and comfortable toilets, and a degree of privacy.

There was thus ample scope for patients' views to be separately represented, even though many doctors, nurses and hospital administrators were aware of the persistence of outmoded practices and attitudes and were doing their best to change them. Miss (later Dame) Muriel Powell, the influential matron of St George's Hospital, London, was prominent in this movement to humanise hospitals and to make them responsive to the changed expectations of patients who no longer saw themselves as recipients of charity. In 1961 she signed, as chairman, the Report of a Sub-committee of the Standing Nursing Advisory Committee on *The Pattern of the In-Patient's Day*. This suggested changes in hospital routine to enable patients to sleep longer in the morning – many hospitals still woke them at 5 a.m. – and to even out some of the peaks of work that harassed patients and nurses alike. Subsequently, Miss Powell worked tirelessly to 'sell' the Report's recommendations to hospitals all over the country.

The Health Service Commissioner

From 1967 onwards a succession of adverse reports and publications on the treatment given to patients in a number of long-stay hospitals (see Chapter 5) turned official attention sharply to the need to have more effective means of monitoring standards and raising them where necessary. The setting up of the Hospital Advisory Service was an immediate consequence of this, and Brian Abel-Smith's suggestion, in *Sans Everything*, of a Hospital Commissioner, or ombudsman, was taken up in Kenneth Robinson's 1968 Green Paper on NHS reorganisation. Robinson suggested two alternatives. When area health boards were set up to run the reorganised NHS, their activities might be brought within the ambit of the Parliamentary Commissioner for Administration, so that he could inquire into matters referred by Members of Parliament within his own terms of reference. The alternative was that there might be a Health Commissioner, appointed perhaps by the Privy Council, who could look into matters complained about and make a recommendation to the relevant area health board.

By 1970, when Richard Crossman's Green Paper appeared, the government were clearly in favour of the establishment of a Health Commissioner, and when the Conservatives returned to power they unhesitatingly adopted the proposal. The 1972 White Paper devoted an appendix to the topic and announced that there would be a Health Service Commissioner for England, one for Wales, and one for Scotland, but that initially at least the three posts would be held by one person, and the work of the Health Service Commissioner would be closely associated with that of the Parliamentary Commissioner for Administration. (In the event, it was decided that the posts of Parliamentary Commissioner and Health Service Commissioner should be held by the same person.) The Commissioner, the White Paper said, would be responsible only for investigating complaints made by or on behalf of patients which had already been made to the responsible health service authorities, but not resolved to the complainant's satisfaction. Access to the Commissioner would be direct, and not, as with the Parliamentary Commissioner, through an MP. The Commissioner would be precluded from investigating any action taken in the course of diagnosis, treatment or clinical care of the individual patient which, in the Commissioner's opinion, was taken solely in the exercise of clinical judgement. Nor would he investigate the actions of general practitioners and other independent contractors, complaints against whom would continue to be handled under the existing statutory provisions. With these exceptions his brief would be to investigate complaints where it was claimed that an individual had suffered injustice or hardship through maladministration, or through failure to provide necessary treatment and care.

The Davies Report

The importance from the patient's point of view of the types of complaint the Commissioner was barred from investigating was made clear when, towards the end of 1973, the Davies Committee produced their Report on Hospital Complaints Procedure. In the list of topics about which members of the public wrote to the Committee, complaints about medical treatment headed the list by a clear margin. The Committee also noted that complaints on clinical matters accounted for nearly half the complaints frc n patients reported by RHBs to the DHSS. The familiar theme ot poor communications ran through many of these complaints, and the Committee expressed the view that even some of the more serious complaints brought to their attention could have been settled if more information or better explanations had been provided. Yet this still left enough complaints about medical care as such for the Committee to feel justified in recommending a new procedure which would offer an alternative to the patient who did not wish to pursue his legal rights and seek compensation in a court of law. The Committee were convinced that many patients, quite apart from not wishing to face the costs of going to law, had no wish to seek damages or punitive action against the doctor concerned. They wished chiefly to ensure that what had happened to them would not happen subsequently to someone else. The Committee suggested there should be established in each region special investigating panels to deal with such complaints, but this suggestion was greeted with hostility by the medical profession – although it was welcomed warmly by the consumer organisations – and no immediate action was taken on it.

The Davies Committee recommended in some detail improvements in the way in which complaints were sometimes handled at ward and hospital level. They drafted a Code of Practice which they hoped the DHSS would adopt, and they called for a record to be kept on each hospital ward of all complaints and suggestions emanating from patients or their relatives.

Community health councils
The Davies Committee also considered the role of the proposed community health councils both in relation to complaints and in the wider sense of consumers' watchdog. The community health councils (CHCs) had first appeared in the 1971 Conservative Consultative Document on NHS reorganisation, and were an expression of Sir Keith Joseph's view that it was right to separate the functions of management and consumer representation. Under existing arrangements, HMCs (and BoGs) were charged with the day-to-day management of the hospital service, but at the same time their members were thought of as in some sense representative of the community and the users of the service. These were difficult roles to combine. With the best will in the world, members found it difficult not to regard consumer criticisms as criticism of their management. Sir Keith's solution was for the area health authorities (AHAs) to manage, and for CHCs to review their performance on behalf of the community, a state of creative tension and, at times perhaps, constructive conflict.

To some extent an afterthought, CHCs attracted a surprising amount of attention as the NHS Reorganisation Bill passed through Parliament, with the result that the government's original proposals were modified. Originally, half the members of a CHC were to be appointed by the relevant local authorities, and half by the AHA, but there was resistance to the idea that AHAs would have the power, to some extent, to choose their own critics, so by the time the Bill came out of Parliament, half the members were to be chosen by local authorities, one-third by voluntary organisations, and the remainder by the regional health authority (RHA). It was also decided that money for CHCs should be provided by the RHAs, rather than the AHAs, and a further amendment to the Bill provided for the possible setting up of a national association of CHCs. The Labour Party disapproved of the principle of separating management from representation, and they and other critics alleged that the consumer watchdogs would turn out to be toothless poodles. However, CHCs were armed with powers to demand information, and AHAs were statutorily obliged to consult them on plans for the future of the service. The official list of matters with which CHCs might appropriately concern themselves grew steadily longer as the Appointed Day approached. As far as individual complaints were concerned, a CHC was expected to advise members of the public on the correct procedure to follow in lodging a complaint, and if necessary to act as a 'patient's friend' in assisting an individual to pursue a complaint competently. A CHC would publish annually a report on its activities and the AHA was obliged to publish its comments and state the action taken on proposals submitted by the CHC.

In line with the views they had expressed during the debates on NHS reorganisation, the incoming Labour government of 1974 promptly produced proposals to strengthen the powers of CHCs and to break down, to some extent, the clear distinction between management and representation. In fact that distinction had already been somewhat eroded, but in her consultative paper of May 1974, *Democracy in the NHS*, Barbara Castle, the new secretary of state, floated the suggestion that CHCs might nominate two members of each AHA. As this suggestion was not well received, the eventual decision was to allow each CHC to send a member to attend AHA meetings with the right to speak but not to vote. *Democracy in the NHS* also announced some firm decisions, including the decision to allow CHCs to appoint their secretaries from outside the NHS if they wished, instead of restricting competition for these posts to NHS officers. This was a potentially important decision, since it opened up these influential posts to individuals who were likely to be more radical in their approach and attitudes than former NHS officers or NHS officers who hoped to return in due course to more senior posts within the service.

Radical criticism
Socially and politically radical criticism of the NHS was mounting during the 1960s and early 1970s, largely as a result of what was seen as a failure to redress disparities between the resources allocated to different patient groups, different parts of the country, and different social classes. The relatively low levels of finance and staffing in the long-stay sectors, and in certain parts of the country, reflected the persistence of a historical pattern which no sufficiently resolute action had been taken to change. The fact that the middle classes tended to get rather better service than the rest of the population reflected rather their own ability to get what they wanted out of the system than any positive discrimination in their favour. Richard Crossman saw the RHBs as the bastions of the *status quo*, and the RHBs themselves as dominated by the consultants. He wanted to reorganise the NHS in such a way that it would be less hospital dominated, less consultant dominated, and more likely to respond to the priority that central government had for some years been urging the service to give to the needs of the elderly, the mentally ill and the mentally handicapped, and to the development of community services. In this Crossman reflected a substantial body of radical opinion, but hostility to the consultants, and what was considered to be their overweening influence on the service, was not confined to radical politicians and their academic allies, but was to be found, during the 1960s, increasingly within certain sectors of the NHS itself.

INDUSTRIAL RELATIONS IN THE NHS

The industrial relations climate in the NHS was traditionally a tranquil one. There were occasional flurries of militant trade union activity, just as there had been in the pre-NHS hospitals, but more often than not these were confined to the mental hospitals, where the great strength lay of the main nursing union, the Confederation of Health Service Employees (COHSE). In the early years of the NHS, it was unusual for nurses in the former voluntary hospitals to be members of a trade union, although union membership was more common, especially among male nurses, in the former local authority hospitals. Several unions, among them the National Union of Public Employees (NUPE), the General and Municipal Workers Union (GMWU), and the Transport and General Workers Union (TGWU), had significant membership among hospital ancillary staffs. It was the ancillary staff who became much more militant in the late 1960s and this culminated in a national strike of hospital ancillary staffs in the early months of 1973.

The strike was precipitated by the government's refusal to relax their current incomes policy in favour of a £4-a-week pay claim by the ancillary staff unions, but the strike was not simply about pay, it was also about relationships at work. This was evident in the marked variation in the intensity of the dispute between one hospital group and another. In some places particular animus was directed at the consultant medical staff and steps were taken to try to prevent the admission and treatment of private patients. Where existing relationships with local management and senior doctors were good, it was almost a case of 'Would it be convenient if we had our strike next week, please?' and no obstacles were placed in the way of the maintenance of essential services. In other cases, management reaped the harvest they had sown in many thoughtless moments over the years, and a group of staff who had traditionally been at the very bottom of the hospital hierarchy learned what it meant to wield power. In areas where the greatest disruption occurred, foul laundry accumulated until it had to be burned as a health hazard; doctors, administrators and senior nurses pushed trolleys; and patients' meals were prepared by whoever happened to be available and willing. Hospitals were discouraged by the DHSS from accepting the help of outside volunteers, as it was felt this would provoke further industrial action.

The management of ancillary services
The background to what could almost be described as 'the revolt of the ancillaries' in 1973 is indicated by the title chosen by Duncan Smith when in 1969 he wrote a treatise on the training of hospital ancillary staff. He called his book *A Forgotten Sector*. The phrase was by then out of date. The spotlight had already turned on the hospital ancillaries in Report No. 29 of the National Board for Prices and Incomes, published two years earlier, but Smith's reference to 'the rather casual way in which the ancillary staff were regarded in the past' was by no means wide of the mark. They were the great unsung army, nearly a quarter of a million of them, men and women, who kept the essential non-medical services of the hospitals going and enabled the professional staff to concentrate on the treatment and care of patients. Report No. 29 made the point that while the earnings of these workers were low, compared with manual workers in industry, this was in large measure because their productivity was also low. The ancillary grades were overmanned and poorly managed. The remedy suggested was the linking of pay to productivity, either through a properly work-studied bonus scheme, or, for the sake of doing something immediately, through a simpler scheme which would reward workers in a particular hospital or department with a 10 per cent bonus in return for a 10 per cent saving in manpower.

Progress in getting workers on to bonus schemes was slow in many parts of the country; there were hospital groups where neither management nor the workers viewed the schemes with any enthusiasm. None the less this Report had a number of important consequences. The unions became more active in the ancillary field; for the first time they could bargain about money at local level. In regions where the RHB pressed HMCs to introduce bonus schemes, a high proportion of the work study officers employed in the service were diverted from other assignments to do the necessary preparatory work. A great deal more attention was paid to the management of ancillary services, and supervisory ratios improved. Duncan Smith's book was an expression of a new concern with training and supervision, which had also been stimulated by the entry of commercial contractors into hospital cleaning and catering a few years before. Finally, workers subject to bonus schemes were likely to examine any change in the organisation or management of their hospital for possible effects on their work and pay. Changes that would have had little significance for workers on a straight hourly rate could be important for workers on bonus. Thus a more calculating, critical workforce was being created at the same time as union organisation at local level was becoming more effective. A further factor in the climate of change affecting ancillary staff at this time was the shedding of non-nursing duties by nurses as a consequence of the implementation of the Salmon Report.

The increased concern with the efficiency of the ancillary workforce was not without its problems. The introduction of bonus schemes to hospitals came at a time when much of industry was turning its back on such schemes, having learned their disadvantages. Managements that already ran a 'tight ship' were penalised because they had difficulty in offering workers the bonus that would accrue from improvements in productivity when productivity was already at a high level and there was little overmanning. At times a rigid insistence on a fixed schedule of duties led to nurses and other professional staff filling in for the ancillary staff so that services to patients should not suffer. An emphasis on efficiency and productivity also made it difficult for hospitals to fulfil their traditional role as an employer of last resort. As the *Economist* put it after the 1973 strike: 'Hospitals provide a niche for the inadequate worker, who finds in them security against the cruel winds of ordinary employment. He is at least doing some work, whereas if dismissed he might fall on Sir Keith Joseph's other plate as a claimant for social security.'

Changes in the professions
The strike was a watershed. On the face of it, the eventual return to work after only token concessions on the part of the government was a

defeat for the unions, and in particular for Alan Fisher of NUPE. On the other hand, the ancillary workers had shown they were a force to be reckoned with and their action also pointed the way to a wider acceptance among health workers generally, including the professions, of industrial action as a means of advancing or protecting their interests. Before many months had passed it was the consultants' turn to invoke industrial action, and the professional nursing organisations were countering aggressive union membership drives by themselves adopting a more militant stance. It was seen that the traditional reluctance of the professions to take action that would jeopardise patients' lives or well-being placed them at a disadvantage compared with other groups that had no such scruples. During the ancillary staff strike there were a number of allegations that patients had lost their lives because of the restrictions on hospital admission, and while some of these might have been difficult to substantiate, at least one union organiser was unperturbed by the fact that this might have been the case. 'You can't make an omelette without breaking eggs', he commented. Yet both NUPE and COHSE had many members with deeply felt reservations about depriving patients of essential services, even in a good and valid cause.

It would perhaps be unfair to conclude that among health service workers generally there was less commitment to their work and to the service in the 1970s than was the case in the years immediately after 1948, and the fact that nurses, for example, are nowadays reluctant to speak of their work as a vocation does not necessarily mean that their attitudes are any less committed. Yet a number of quite obvious changes have taken place in the terms in which nurses, and doctors too, see their work. In the early years, in spite of Whitley Council agreements limiting working hours to forty-eight, many nurses were working fifty-two hours a week or more. By 1974 the forty-hour week was the rule. By the 1970s empty or half-empty nurses' homes – and others turned over to alternative uses – bore witness to a trend for more nurses to live out. By 1970 it was uncommon for a nurse to give up her work, or her training, on marriage – at least until she started a family. In many hospitals in 1948 the nurse who married was expected to resign, or abandon her training. All these changes meant that work for the average nurse in 1974 filled less of her time and had a less central place in her life than was the case with her counterpart in 1948. With more free time, more money to spend, living away from the hospital, she might well have brought to her work a freshness and a breadth of interests that it was difficult for the nurse who lived and breathed in the hospital atmosphere twenty-four hours a day to bring, but equally it was easier for her to regard nursing as just another job, a way of making a living, rather than as something rather special, calling for dedication out of the ordinary, and a measure of self-sacrifice.

CHANGES IN SEXUAL MORES

The Family Planning Act

In experiencing increasing consumer militancy and a new assertiveness among rank and file workers the NHS mirrored changes in the wider society. The important changes that took place during its first twenty-six years in general attitudes towards sexual experience and behaviour obliged the NHS not only to modify some of its personnel practices, and to treat the private lives of staff as very much more their own business, but also to provide a whole new range of facilities as a result of such legislation as the Abortion Act and the National Health Service (Family Planning) Act, both of which received the Royal Assent in 1967. The Family Planning Act, as it is generally known, gave powers to local health authorities, subject to the approval of the Minister of Health, to make arrangements, either directly or through voluntary organisations, for the giving of advice on contraception, for the medical examination of persons seeking advice, and for the supply of contraceptive substances and appliances. These very wide powers replaced the authority given by section 28 of the National Health Service Act to give such a service to those who required it on medical grounds. Under the 1967 Act there was no such restriction and the service could be given to those who required it whether on medical or social grounds. The Act made no distinction between the married and the unmarried.

In many areas local authorities chose to make arrangements with the Family Planning Association (FPA) rather than to provide a family planning service themselves. Often the local authority provided the building and the FPA the staff, with an agreed proportion of the running costs – 100 per cent in some cases, in others less – being reimbursed to the FPA by the local authority. There were cases where, in spite of the failure of the Act to distinguish between the married and the unmarried, local authorities refused to reimburse the FPA for the costs of advising unmarried women. In the first three years after the Act came into force, FPA clinics increased from 613 to 1,023, and seventy-one local authorities had started their own clinics. In addition to the setting up of clinics, the 1967 Act made it possible for local authorities to make a more determined effort to get family planning advice to those who were in most need of it by setting up a domiciliary family planning service. In other cases, a service was set up within a maternity hospital or maternity department by arrangement with the hospital authority.

The Abortion Act

The Abortion Act 1967 was one of the most controversial manifestations of what was sometimes termed the permissive society, although there were others, including Roy Jenkins, Home Secretary at the time, who talked rather of the 'compassionate society'. For more than thirty years the Abortion Law Reform Association had campaigned for a widening of the grounds on which abortion might legally be carried out. In the event, the Act was the outcome of a Private Member's Bill introduced by a Liberal MP, David Steel. The Act confirmed that abortion was lawful if the continuance of the pregnancy would involve risk to the life of the pregnant woman, but went on to widen the grounds on which abortion could lawfully be performed to include the risk of injury to the social or mental health of the pregnant woman or any existing children of the family. The Act provided that abortions should only be carried out in NHS hospitals or other premises approved by the minister, that they should be notified to the chief medical officer of the Ministry of Health, or Scottish Home and Health Department. A conscience clause was inserted for the benefit of Roman Catholic and other nurses who might object to being required to assist at abortion operations as part of their employment.

The Act relieved a vast amount of individual suffering and largely put out of business the back-street abortionists who had been responsible for so many deaths in the past. It focused attention on the need for more widespread contraceptive advice and facilities and it stimulated research into simpler and safer techniques of abortion. All this was, however, at the cost of some strain on NHS facilities and staff. In parts of the country it was difficult to staff operating theatres for abortion lists because of the conscience clause. The solution of setting up special abortion centres staffed by doctors and nurses who saw the work as a humanitarian opportunity rather than an affront to conscience was widely discussed but the only centres set up were those created outside the NHS by voluntary or profit-making organisations. In those areas where the consultant gynaecologists were unwilling to carry out abortions under the terms of the Act, women turned in large numbers to private clinics which had been licensed by the minister, and soon after the passage of the Act allegations were heard that the private sector was abusing its provisions, and that lax interpretation of the grounds laid down amounted in effect to abortion on demand. In addition, doctors in private practice, and clinic proprietors, were said to be making excessive profits both from British women unable to secure abortions under the NHS and from women coming from overseas to secure abortions that would not be available to them under the laws of their own countries. For these and other reasons the government set up in 1972 a Committee on the Working of the Abortion Act under the chairmanship of Mrs Justice Lane. When the Lane Committee reported in 1974 they gave the Act itself a clean bill of health and did not consider that any amendment was required. Any problems in the working of the Act could be dealt with by administrative and professional action.

The Committee viewed with disquiet the fact that in 1971 nearly half the resident women having abortions were treated in the private sector. They had no hesitation in viewing this as an indication of the inadequacy of the service provided by NHS hospitals, and pointed out that since the Abortion Act, the abortion of women on the grounds laid down came within the scope of the secretary of state's statutory obligation under the National Health Service Act to provide hospital and specialist services 'to such extent as he considers necessary to meet all reasonable requirements'. Statistics published in the Report showed that a woman's chances of getting an NHS abortion varied considerably according to the region in which she lived. In the East Anglian Region, 16·7 per cent of discharges and deaths from gynaecological beds were of notifiable abortion cases. At the other extreme, the figure for the Birmingham Region was 5·7 per cent.

Apart from the conscientious arguments against abortion as such, some gynaecologists were unhappy about the Act because they felt the beds being filled by abortion cases were badly needed for the treatment of patients with other distressing or life-threatening conditions. It was therefore of interest that the Lane Committee found no evidence that other patients had suffered, either in terms of not being able to get treatment, or having to wait a long time for it, in those regions with high abortion rates. Where many abortions were performed, the length of stay in hospital tended to be short, and this seemed to have enabled gynaecological departments in some regions to deal with a large number of abortion cases while maintaining an increase in their other work, with some improvement in the total service offered. This showed what could be achieved with good organisation, efficient use of resources, and close co-operation with domiciliary health and social services.

THE CHRONICALLY SICK, THE DISABLED AND THE ELDERLY

A further manifestation of the compassionate society was the passage in 1970 of the Chronically Sick and Disabled Persons Act. Like the Abortion Act, this was the result of a Private Member's Bill. In introducing his Bill, Alfred Morris had the support of a number of voluntary organisations which had been campaigning for some years for better services and facilities for the disabled. The success of medicine in keeping alive people who in earlier times would have perished meant there were an increasing number of disabled people in the community. By 1970 there were at least 3 million adults who were disabled in some degree, upwards of 1·25 million adults under the age of 65 disabled severely, and 200,000 families with a severely disabled member, but without an inside lavatory. One in five of the severely disabled, Alfred Morris told the House of Commons, lived alone without the help of welfare services.

The Act laid on local authorities a duty to ascertain how many disabled people lived in their areas, to make adequate services available, and to ensure that those who needed services were aware of them. The facilities local authorities were called on to provide for the disabled ranged from help in adapting the home of a disabled person to meet his special needs, to making arrangements for him to have a holiday. Further provisions of the Act required that any building open to the public should have means of access and toilet facilities suitable for disabled people, that various advisory committees to the government should have disabled persons among their members, and that hospital authorities should ensure, as far as was practicable, that the young chronic sick were not cared for in wards otherwise devoted to the care of the aged. Young chronically sick patients were often admitted to geriatric wards simply because there were no other facilities for long-term care. The lack of specific facilities for the young chronic sick within the NHS had prompted the founding of the voluntary Cheshire Homes to meet their needs, but now the Act required hospital authorities to make similar efforts to provide an environment suitable for patients who, though physically disabled, were usually mentally alert and of good intelligence.

The new duties laid on local authorities came at a time when they were reorganising to implement the Local Authority Social Services Act of 1970. This in turn had stemmed from the Seebohm Report of 1968, which had recommended the setting up in each major local authority of a unified social service department with its own director, embracing the former local authority welfare and children's departments, and social work elements from the health, education and housing departments. At the same time, local authorities were also having to cope with the provisions of the Health Services and Public Health Act of 1968. This was a ragbag Act designed largely to tidy up a number of legislative loose ends, but buried in all the detail was the important section 45 conferring on local authorities a duty to provide for the general welfare of old people, over and above their duties to provide various specific services under previous legislation. This section was complemented by section 13, which for the first time made it a duty of local authorities to provide home help services; previously they had been empowered but not obliged to do so. Section 13 also empowered local authorities to provide laundry services. Both these services were likely to benefit mainly the elderly.

Sections 13 and 45 did not come into operation until April 1971 and meanwhile the Department of Health circularised authorities asking them to review the welfare needs of the elderly in their areas and to work out means of meeting them in partnership with voluntary organisations. The circular went on to urge local authorities to publicise their services and, where all needs could not be met, to select priority groups, such as people over 75, the housebound, the recently bereaved, or areas where there was a high concentration of elderly people. Many authorities were slow to take action after section 45 came into effect, partly because of the disruption created by the Seebohm reorganisation, but also because while the Act created new duties, it did not also create new resources to discharge them. Similar considerations created difficulties with the implementation of the Chronically Sick and Disabled Persons Act, and prompted Alfred Morris to point out that authorities that dragged their feet were dragging them at the expense of those with no feet to drag.

The particular concern with the welfare of the disabled and the elderly exemplified by these two pieces of legislation reflected not only the values of the compassionate society, but also the changing age structure of the population. The fact that implementing these Acts fell to a large extent to the new social service departments of local authorities rather than to the local authority arm of the NHS underlined the success of social workers in claiming for their own what was in many cases part of the former empire of the medical officer of health. Thus was defined the boundary between health and social services which after 1974 was to pose problems of collaboration and co-ordination between health and local authorities.

9
Reorganisation – Launched on a Sea of Words

Never put to sea in a storm. Hesiod's advice to mariners

The National Health Service was barely established when suggestions for reorganisation were put forward. The Guillebaud Report, by dismissing these as premature, and by pointing out what the service needed above all was a period of stability, pushed the debate into the background for a while, but by the early 1960s the topic was again to the fore. The chief change that was felt to be necessary by almost all who put forward schemes of radical reform was the unification of the three branches of the service then administered by hospital boards and committees, local health authorities, and the executive councils. It was sometimes also assumed that the local authority health services would bring with them into any unified structure those social services – chiefly welfare homes and services for the aged, the mentally ill and the mentally handicapped – which in many authorities were administered by the medical officer of health and were the responsibility of a health and welfare committee of the council.

THE PORRITT REPORT

The year 1962 saw the publication of a Report which brought together much of the thinking that had been going on and gave a new impetus to discussion. The Porritt Committee were set up by the Royal Colleges of Physicians, Surgeons, Obstetricians and Gynaecologists, and General Practitioners, and their Scottish counterparts, together with the British Medical Association and the Society of Medical Officers of Health. Their terms of reference were 'to review the provision of medical services to the public, and their organisation, in the light of ten years' experience of the National Health Service, and to make recommendations'. All the members of the Committee were doctors, but evidence was taken from a wide range of organisations and individuals, and a public opinion survey was conducted by Gallup Polls (Social Survey) Ltd, to find out what the general public thought of the NHS. The findings of this survey were printed as an appendix to the Porritt Report.

The Porritt Report proposed the unification of the three parts of the NHS under area health boards, each serving a defined population, the ideal population and the total number of boards to be determined after further research. All existing health services would be brought into this system, with the exception of the teaching hospitals, which would retain their existing boards of governors, responsible directly to the Ministry of Health. Regional hospital boards would be abolished but area health boards would join together to create regional planning committees to deal with those services that could only be planned economically over a wider area. In order to carry out its duties effectively each area health board should have a number of subsidiary councils responsible to it for the day-to-day administration of individual services, viz.: (1) a general medical, dental, pharmaceutical and ophthalmic services council; (2) a hospital services council; (3) a preventive and social health services council; and (4) an occupational health services council. Each board would be given a high degree of autonomy in administering and planning the health services, and membership of the boards would include representatives from all the health service professions. In addition, each subordinate council would be served by a professional advisory committee consisting of representatives of those professions actively engaged in the service for which it was responsible, and these professional advisory committees would themselves set up an area advisory committee to advise the area health board on professional issues. At national level the Central Health Services Council would be replaced by an advisory committee consisting of the chosen representatives of the professions rather than people appointed by the minister.

The Committee recognised that there was a strong feeling within the medical profession that the health service should be taken 'out of politics' and placed under the control of an independent corporation. The British Broadcasting Corporation was the example often cited. However, it was pointed out that this was not a realistic aspiration for a service with little or no income of its own. Such a corporation would – unless the whole financial basis of the NHS were changed – be merely a spending agency for a very substantial sum of public money. Moreover, other nationalised undertakings which had been placed under the control of independent public corporations remained answerable to a minister for broad policy and were subject to questions in Parliament; they were by no means removed from the sphere of politics. The Porritt Committee went further. There were positive advantages in direct ministerial responsibility. The ability to have questions raised in Parliament had at times been useful both to the public and to the professions. A minister too was likely to be more sensitive to public opinion than a nationalised board. However, there was a need to bring governmental responsibilities for health matters together in one department, under one minister of Cabinet rank. At the time, nine government departments provided health services of one kind or another in addition to those provided by the Ministry of Health and the Scottish Home and Health Department. These included the school health service, which was under the Ministry of Education, and medical services run by the Ministries of Labour, Housing and Local Government, Pensions, Agriculture and Fisheries, and the Home Office.

Inevitably, with a Committee so constituted, there were examples of special pleading. The 'chief officer' of each area health board must be a doctor; the social workers in the 'department of social health' to be attached to each major general hospital would come under the control of a doctor. The problems of general practitioners, then the most restive group in the profession, were given close attention. While recording a 'firm view that both the capitation method of payment and the Pool system at present fall short of providing the best incentives and encouragement to good general practice', the Committee were unable to suggest any better system. Salaried service was seen as a threat to professional freedom, and it was felt that a fee-for-service system would be complicated, rigid and involve a great deal of book-keeping. It would also be open to abuse. Above all, there was repeated emphasis on the need to safeguard private practice, erected in the concluding section into a 'fundamental principle' – along with 'our firm opposition to any system which could leave a learned profession at the mercy of party politics', and the need for administrative unification of the service.

'THE SHAPE OF HOSPITAL MANAGEMENT IN 1980 ?'

In view of the growing agreement that the three parts of the NHS needed to be brought together, there was something a little anachronistic about the title of a report, *The Shape of Hospital Management in 1980 ?*, which was compiled by a joint working party of the King's Fund and the Institute of Hospital Administrators and published as a discussion document rather than a policy document in 1967. It was not that the working party did not recognise that the three parts must draw more closely together and that by the 1980s hospitals would be part of an integrated structure; it was rather that they assumed that the district general hospital would be the basic management unit, and the associated community health and welfare services played a clearly subordinate part in their deliberations.

For such a management unit the working party envisaged a management structure of classical simplicity. There would be, to replace the existing hospital management committee, a much smaller district hospital board, consisting of a chairman and seven other members. The chief executive officer of the district hospital would be a general manager, who would be a member of the district hospital board, as also would be the chairman of the community service medical advisory committee and the community service patients' advisory committee. The chairman of the district hospital board would, unlike chairmen of HMCs, be paid an honorarium for his services.

The general manager would be assisted by four directors of service: (1) director of medical and paramedical services; (2) director of nursing services; (3) director of finance and statistical services; and (4) director of general services. A hospital medical services advisory committee would be appointed by the senior clinical staff to advise the director of medical and paramedical services.

The '1980' Report is of interest because it contained several ideas which came to the fore during subsequent discussions. The payment of chairmen and the general reduction in the size of committees and boards were features of the reorganisation as it took place in 1974; the notion of a general manager, or chief executive, was at one stage canvassed, but did not find favour, particularly with medical and nursing interests. In view of the pattern of team management that did emerge, it is worth noting the comment by the '1980' working party that 'We do not accept that it is good management to have a number of senior officers all of whom are considered equal and responsible only to a committee of management'. The working party of course rejected the view of the Salmon Committee that the chief nursing officer should be responsible directly to the management committee rather than through the group secretary.

The '1980' Report was thus as much an administrative report as the Porritt Report was a medical document. Although the membership of the working party had included one doctor (Professor John Anderson), the proposals, and especially the suggestions for a chief executive and a director of medical and paramedical services, were largely unacceptable to the medical profession. On the other hand, when the Cogwheel Report on the Organisation of Medical Work in Hospitals appeared (see Chapter 7), it included a recommendation that the chairman of the medical executive committee should perform functions, on a part-time basis, not dissimilar to those suggested in '1980' for the director of medical and paramedical services.

THE FIRST GREEN PAPER

The following year, 1968, the initiative passed to the Ministry of Health with the publication of the first Green Paper on NHS reorganisation. The previous autumn the minister, Kenneth Robinson, had told the House of Commons that he had begun a full and careful examination of the administrative structure of the NHS, and in July 1968 he published his conclusions as *The Administrative Structure of Medical and Related Services in England and Wales*. The then novel device of a Green Paper was chosen to indicate that the proposals were for discussion and consultation and did not represent, as a White Paper might be expected to represent, a firm commitment by the government to the policies expressed. Widespread discussion followed the publication of the Green Paper and it became clear that although there was general acceptance of the fundamental point that the three parts of the NHS should be unified, this general agreement did not extend to many of the detailed proposals, such as the sharp reduction in the numbers of committees and boards and in the numbers of people required to give voluntary service on these committees and boards.

The Green Paper envisaged the replacement of the existing structure by forty to fifty area boards which would combine the functions of hospital authorities, local health authorities (as far as personal health services were concerned) and executive councils. It was suggested that these area boards – which as far as the hospital service was concerned would replace both RHBs and HMCs – might either be specially constituted bodies responsible directly to the Minister of Health, or, if the Royal Commission on Local Government, which was then sitting, recommended a suitable structure for local government, they might be set up as committees of new-type local authorities. It was important, the Green Paper argued, that the internal organisation of the area board should not reflect existing divisions between hospital and community services, but should mark a clean break with the present. Standing committees should be few and should be kept small in the interests of efficiency and of observing the proper distinction between the policy-forming responsibilities of members and the management functions of officers. While it would not be appropriate to have, say, a hospital services committee or a general practitioner services committee, there might be, for example, a planning committee, responsible for planning all parts of the service. Headquarters departments of the area board should similarly reflect functional divisions, such as planning, logistics, finance, staffing and administrative support services, rather than the responsibilities of existing authorities.

With this form of organisation the senior officers of the area board appointed as directors of the four or five functional departments would together make up a small executive, which would meet frequently and be collectively responsible to the board for advising on objectives and policies, for organising the services of the area, for executing the board's policies, and for maintaining the standard of service. The chief administrative officer would have as his principal task the co-ordination of the work of the directors and he would preside at meetings of the executive. He would be the board's principal adviser on all non-professional matters and would also be director of the secretariat. The chief medical officer, who would also have direct access to the board, would be the principal adviser on all medical professional matters and would be director of the department dealing with the planning and operation of services.

THE SECOND GREEN PAPER

Later in 1968 the government departments concerned with social services were reorganised and the Department of Health and Social Security (DHSS) was created with a secretary of state, of Cabinet rank, at its head. Richard Crossman was appointed to the new post, and he quickly announced that it was his intention to prepare revised proposals for NHS reorganisation taking into account many of the comments and criticisms that had been made following publication of the first Green Paper. In particular there seemed to be wide support for the view that to have forty to fifty area boards would lead to areas too small for planning purposes and too large for effective management. In preparing Green Paper II, which appeared in 1970, Crossman also had the advantage of having to hand the Report of the Royal Commission on Local Government, published in the summer of 1969.

Green Paper II, which was entitled *The Future Structure of the National Health Service* and published in 1970, announced three firm decisions by the government as a result of the earlier discussions and the Report of the Royal Commission, and put forward a further series of proposals for public debate. The three firm decisions were:

(a) that the National Health Service would not be administered by local government but by area health authorities directly responsible to the secretary of state and closely associated with local authorities;

(*b*) that the boundary between the health service and the personal social services provided by local authorities should be determined by the skills of the providers rather than the needs of the users, i.e. health authorities would be responsible for services where the primary skill needed was that of the health professions, while the local authorities would be responsible for services where the primary skill was social care or support;

(*c*) the geographical boundaries of the health service areas should match those of the new local authorities; there would thus be ninety or thereabouts, compared with forty to fifty proposed in Green Paper I.

The second of these three firm decisions was influenced by the publication about the same time as Green Paper I of the Seebohm Report on Local Authority and Allied Personal Social Services. This report had envisaged the creation under each major local authority of a unified social service department with a director of social services at its head, bringing together existing children's departments with social work elements from health and welfare, housing, education and other local authority departments, as well as possibly social workers from the hospital service. The government had accepted the main recommendations of the Seebohm Report, which were in due course implemented in the Local Authority Social Services Act 1970. Whether or not the Seebohm reorganisation of personal social services represented in the long run an improvement in the service rendered to individuals and the community – and like most such questions, this remains open to dispute – it undoubtedly represented a triumph for the professional aspirations of social workers and a blow to those who felt that the division between health and welfare services created at least as many problems as did the divisions between the three parts of the NHS itself.

The boundary between the health and social services required by such groups as the aged and the mentally disturbed had always been difficult to draw and both health and local authorities tended to blame each other for not providing the necessary facilities. One of the more powerful arguments for local authorities to take over the health service was that the same authority would be responsible for providing residential homes and hostels as was responsible for providing hospital care, and planning of a comprehensive range of provision would then be possible uninfluenced by the consideration that one service was funded directly by the Exchequer and the other partly from local rates. The government's acceptance of the Seebohm recommendations also laid the foundation for much bitterness among medical officers of health at the time of NHS reorganisation, for after 1970 many of them lost substantial sections of their departments to the new directors of social services and they viewed with a jaundiced eye any further blows to their status and managerial role.

Green Paper II, in addition to increasing the number of area health authorities (AHAs) – the term 'authority' was substituted for 'board' ·without comment or explanation – met the criticism that the areas would be too small for planning purposes by proposing the creation of fourteen or more regional health councils. These would advise the area health authorities and the secretary of state on the planning of services and would take responsibility for organising postgraduate medical education. They were not seen as part of the chain of command stretching from the secretary of state to the area health authorities, who would be answerable directly to the Department of Health. The chairman and some members of the regional council would be appointed by the secretary of state. Others would be appointed by the constituent health authorities, the professions and the related university.

It was proposed that one-third of the members of the area health authorities should be appointed by the health professions, one-third by the relevant local authorities, and one-third, plus the chairman, by the secretary of state. It was felt that the local authority membership would introduce an element of local democratic participation and at the same time promote co-ordination between health and local authority services Chairmen of AHAs would be paid part-time salaries.

The decision that the health areas should have the same boundaries as the areas of the major local authorities meant that they would serve populations varying from about 200,000 to about 1·3 million; in many cases therefore there would be more than one health district, if such were defined as the catchment area of a district general hospital. It was proposed that in such areas the AHA should set up district committees – it was expected there would be about 200 of these – and such a committee would consist of a chairman and members drawn half from the AHA and half from people living or working in the district who were not members of the AHA itself. The district committees were not seen as a further statutory tier and no functions were to be delegated to them by statute. They would, however, exercise general supervision over the running of services at district level, and would help keep the AHA in touch with problems with the local health services encountered by people in the districts.

The emphasis laid on the need for local participation and for close links with related local authority services made it obvious that the government must have considered carefully the possibility of giving the new local authorities, to be established as a result of the recommendations of the Royal Commission, responsibility for running the health service. Two main reasons were given for the rejection of this solution. 'First, the professions believe that only a service administered by special bodies on which the professions are represented can provide a proper assurance of clinical freedom. Secondly, the independent financial resources available to local authorities are not sufficient to enable them to take over responsibility for the whole health service.' In this context, 'the professions' meant, overwhelmingly, the medical profession.

Although Green Paper I had covered England and Wales, Green Paper II was for England only. A separate Green Paper was produced for Wales, on broadly similar lines, but taking account of administrative devolution to the Welsh Office and the special geographical circumstances of Wales. Discussions on the reorganisation of the Scottish health service also proceeded independently in parallel.

THE CONSULTATIVE DOCUMENT

When the Conservatives came to power in late 1970 Richard Crossman was succeeded as Secretary of State for Social Services by Sir Keith Joseph, who published a Consultative Document embodying his proposals for NHS reorganisation in May 1971. 'We are perhaps in danger', he wrote in his Foreword, 'of a surfeit of plans and prospectuses: there must be early decisions, so that enthusiasm for reform does not wither away.'

The Consultative Document recorded a wide measure of agreement on the basic principle of administrative unification of the existing tripartite structure and on the principle that the new area health authorities should have the same geographical boundaries as the reformed local authorities. 1 April 1974 was fixed as the date on which both sets of new authorities should come into being. Sir Keith claimed that the essence of his proposals for the health service – and their basic difference from earlier proposals – was the emphasis placed on effective management. 'The importance of good management in making the best use of resources can hardly be overstated', he wrote. So the regional tier was firmly established as part of a classical chain-of-command structure, passing orders to the area authorities and receiving from them accounts of how they had discharged their delegated responsibilities.

The Document announced that AHA members would be chosen for 'management ability' rather than as representatives of various interests. The more detailed account of the way in which these members would be appointed which followed this categorical statement gave rise to doubts as to whether it really meant what it said, but none the less health service administrators found disturbing the implication that part-time, unpaid members were expected to 'manage' the health service, as distinct from setting policies within which it would be managed by the officers. Sir Keith proposed that the chairman and all the members of regional health authorities (RHAs) would be appointed by the secretary of state, after consultation with interested organisations. The secretary of state would also appoint the chairman of each AHA, but the members – who would number fourteen or fifteen in addition to the chairman – would be appointed as follows: (a) some by the corresponding local authority; (b) one by the relevant university (two in a teaching area); (c) the remainder by the RHA after consultations; these members would include at least two doctors and one nurse or midwife.

In Sir Keith's proposals Richard Crossman's district committees became community health councils (CHCs), charged with representing the views of the public to the health authorities, but firmly barred from any part in the management of the service. They thus became purely and simply consumer watchdogs. Sir Keith retained the principle of payment for chairmen of authorities, and announced that strong professional advisory machinery would be established at both regional and area levels.

Two topics which required further consideration were the arrangements to be made to ensure effective co-ordination between the new health authorities and the local authority departments for social services, environmental control, housing and education, and the internal management structures of the regional and area health authorities. The Consultative Document announced that special studies would be mounted in these areas.

The Document discussed briefly arrangements for the administration of the family practitioner services, and the position of the teaching hospitals. AHAs were to be required to set up statutory committees to administer the contracts of family doctors, dentists, pharmacists and opticians, and in this form the old insurance committees, which became in 1948 the executive councils, would survive into the new structure, albeit under the overall control of the AHAs. A similar willingness to make concessions to established interests was demonstrated in the Appendix which described the 'special arrangements for districts where there are substantial facilities for medical and dental clinical teaching', in other words the districts served by the teaching hospitals. It was made clear that the teaching districts would be administered as parts of the areas in which they were situated, but among other provisions to maintain the 'individual identity and historic traditions' of the teaching hospitals there would be special financial arrangements and a district committee to manage the services of the district. It was promised that arrangements would be made for one or two members of existing boards of governors and university hospital management committees to be appointed to each of the area authorities concerned and to each teaching district committee. (University hospital management committees were created under the Health Services and Public Health Act 1968, which made it possible for a hospital not formerly designated as a teaching hospital to be so designated and to have representatives of the relevant university added to its HMC. In the next year or two advantage was taken of this provision to designate several new teaching hospitals without removing them from the control of their RHB.)

THE WHITE PAPER

The next formal stage in the debate was the issue in August 1972 of a White Paper on National Health Service Reorganisation: England. The White Paper contained little that was new and built firmly on the foundations laid in the Consultative Document. The RHAs would be based on the fourteen planning regions already established for the hospital service. The AHAs would share the boundaries of the new nonmetropolitan counties and metropolitan districts. London local government had been reorganised in 1963 and was not to be reorganised again in 1974, so the White Paper announced special arrangements for London which meant that while health areas would be formed out of single London boroughs or groups of boroughs, the health districts would not always follow the borough boundaries. The special arrangements for London included keeping in being the existing boards of governors for the postgraduate hospitals until such time as these hospitals – highly specialised institutions often drawing patients from all over the country and from overseas – became sufficiently closely associated with other hospitals and services in the vicinity to make it feasible for them to be administered by the new health authorities.

The teaching hospital lobby had been hard at work, and in addition to this concession to the postgraduate teaching hospitals, the White Paper replaced the Consultative Document's plan for 'teaching districts', subordinate to AHAs but with some special privileges, with the notion of the 'teaching area' managed by an area health authority specially constituted and to be known as an AHA(T). The AHA(T)s would, however, be accountable to the RHA in the same way as other AHAs. One of the privileges accruing to an AHA(T) would be that it would employ its own senior medical and dental staff. Elsewhere, senior doctors and dentists would be employed by the RHA, as in the existing NHS.

The date for NHS reorganisation was reaffirmed as 1 April 1974, to coincide with the reorganisation of local government. Reports of the studies being made of detailed management arrangements and of arrangements to secure close collaboration between health and local authorities were still awaited, although some of the ideas being developed in the course of the management study were set out as an Appendix to the White Paper, and the White Paper announced that the NHS Reorganisation Bill would seek to lay on both types of authority a statutory duty to collaborate with each other. A further Appendix gave details of the government's proposal to establish a Health Service Commissioner to deal with complaints against the NHS (see Chapter 8 for fuller discussion of this aspect of reorganisation).

The White Paper, Sir Keith told the public in his Foreword, was about administration, not about treatment and care. 'But the purpose behind the changes proposed is a better, more sensitive service to the public . . . The White Paper demonstrates the Government's concern to see that arrangements are evolved under which a more coherent and smoothly interlocking range of services will develop for all the needs of the population.' The White Paper went on to describe how, in order that imbalances between different parts of the service should be corrected and priorities selected and regularly reviewed, the DHSS would plan the broad strategy and monitor the performance of the health service, the regions would plan within this strategy and supervise the work of the areas, while the areas would be responsible for the most detailed level of planning and for operational control of services. Already the Consultative Document had laid down the principle 'that throughout the new administrative structure there should be a clear definition and allocation of responsibilities; that there should be maximum delegation downwards, matched by accountability upwards; and that a sound management structure should be created at all levels'. The White Paper Appendix on management arrangements showed that the application of this principle was being worked out in considerable detail and there was likely to be much more prescription by the central department than had been the case in 1948.

The new regional and area authorities would be appointed, the White Paper stated, as soon as possible after the necessary legislation was passed. They would therefore be in existence in 'shadow' form for some months before they took over responsibility from existing authorities. Meanwhile, joint liaison committees (JLCs) were already being established, one for each new health area, with memberships drawn from the existing authorities. The JLCs were to prepare the way for the new authorities, making recommendations on the division of areas into districts and on staffing and accommodation requirements, and they were also to play an important part in keeping NHS staff informed on the progress of reorganisation and how it was likely to affect them.

THE MANAGEMENT ARRANGEMENTS

The White Paper was rapidly followed by publication of the full report of the study group on *Management Arrangements for the Reorganised National Health Service*, which soon became known as the 'Grey Book'. The small study group had worked under the guidance of a much larger steering committee drawn both from the DHSS and NHS authorities, and with the advice of the international management consultants McKinsey & Co. Inc., and the Health Services Organisation Research Unit of Brunel University, headed by Professor Elliot Jaques. Even at this stage the government did not wish to commit themselves too firmly on detail and so the report was designated a discussion document. Time for discussion was, however, running out, and most of the important recommendations in the Grey Book quickly became firm decisions. In any case, opinion had already been canvassed on many of the topics covered as a result first of a study carried out by Maurice Naylor, secretary of Sheffield RHB, which was published by the Institute of Health Service Administrators in mid-1971 under the title *Organisation of Area Health Services*, and then by means of informal circulation of what the management arrangements study group termed a 'first hypothesis'. These feelers had established beyond doubt that a system of management based on the concept of a chief executive, as outlined in the '1980' Report, would not be acceptable, and the Grey Book therefore based the management of the NHS on the concept of a team of equals, reaching decisions by consensus.

At district, the operational level of the service, the district management team (DMT) would consist of a district community physician (DCP), a district nursing officer (DNO), a district finance officer (DFO), a district administrator (DA), together with two elected medical representatives, one a consultant, the other a general practitioner. The title 'district community physician' was the term approved in the Report of the Working Party on Medical Administrators (Hunter Report), published in 1972, and implied a full-time medical administrator, skilled in identifying the health needs of the population served, and in reviewing the effectiveness of the services provided. The title 'district nursing officer' did not imply, as many members of the public subsequently assumed, a background in district nursing, but signified the head of the nursing service in the district.

In an area with more than one district, the area team of officers (ATO) would consist of the area medical officer (AMO) – the area counterpart of the DCP – the area nursing officer (ANO), area treasurer (AT), and area administrator (AA); in a single-district area these would have added to them two elected medical members, one a consultant and one a general practitioner, and be known as the area management team (AMT). In England it was laid down that the district chief officers would *not* be the subordinates of their area counterparts. There would be no line management relationship between them. The DMT would be directly accountable to the AHA. The area officers would be the AHA's principal advisers, they would have important planning responsibilities, and they would monitor the work of the districts, reporting when necessary to the AHA, but having no power to direct district officers to take or not take any particular action. This sophisticated, and many felt unworkable, relationship was peculiar to England. In Wales, Scotland and Northern Ireland, things were arranged in a more straightforward manner, with a line relationship between area officers and their district counterparts.

It is not entirely clear why England ventured on a path so fraught with possibilities of tension and conflict. A certain unworldliness among some of the academic advisers to the study group, which tempted them to believe that chief officers who had been influential, even powerful, as group secretaries and chief nursing officers, would readily relinquish the habit of command if required to do so by fiat from the DHSS, may have been a factor. On the other hand, with the sharp reduction in the number of authorities, it was inevitable that many existing chief officers would have to be accommodated in district rather than area posts, and it was thus in their interests to secure the maximum autonomy for these posts. It seems likely, too, that a number of areas were divided on the recommendation of the joint liaison committees into two or more districts that it might have been wiser to leave as single-district areas, and this also reflected among other factors the desire of existing chief officers to protect their future interests. In both cases a good deal of trouble was laid up for the future.

THE NATIONAL HEALTH SERVICE STAFF COMMISSION

A Staff Advisory Committee, which on the passage of the National Health Service Reorganisation Act in the summer of 1973 became the National Health Service Staff Commission, was set up in April 1972 to supervise the appointment and transfer of staff to the new NHS authorities. Similar, but separate, bodies were set up in Wales and Scotland. On the whole the transfer of the great majority of staff, who after the Appointed Day would be performing much the same duties as they performed before, proceeded smoothly, although the variety of conditions of service which existed between local authorities themselves, and between local authorities and the hospital service, gave rise to some difficulties and friction. The same cannot be said of the arrangements for the appointment of senior staff to the new authorities. The Commission were indeed faced with a formidable and delicate task, but they did not distinguish themselves in their handling of it, and to a substantial degree the widespread demoralisation of the NHS in the early months after the reorganisation must be laid at their door.

The task was to devise means of appointing senior officers to regional, are and district posts in such a way that the new authorities would be well served by able and efficient officers and all those reasonably entitled to be considered for such posts would feel that justice had been done to their claims. Interestingly, one of the themes about which a good deal had been heard from the DHSS in the year or two leading up to reorganisation was the need to improve the standard of personnel management in the NHS; here then was an opportunity to set an example of good practice in such matters. The staff organisations kept a watchful eye on the proceedings of the Staff Commission, and seemed particularly anxious to ensure that local authority and executive council staff should be assured of equal consideration with officers from the hospital service. The secretary of state, Sir Keith Joseph, gave public assurances that these groups of staff would receive their fair share of the top posts, and there would be no hospital takeover.

Politically, it was no doubt necessary to give this assurance, but it implied that factors other than ability, experience and qualifications would be taken into account. The pre-1974 NHS was dominated, both in terms of numbers of staff and of expenditure, by the hospital service, and thus experience of large-scale management was, apart from a few of the largest local authorities, almost entirely confined to hospital officers. In fair and open competition it was almost inevitable that there would be what could be seen as a 'hospital takeover', so the secretary of state's remarks, whilst reassuring to local authority interests, made hospital officers feel that the scales were likely to be weighted against them.

The Staff Commission agreed with the staff organisations that initially at least applications for the most senior posts would only be considered from staff already working within the merging parts of the NHS. As far as the majority of posts were concerned it is doubtful whether many candidates of suitable calibre and with relevant experience would have presented themselves from outside the NHS even if competition had been thrown open from the start. In one or two specialised fields, perhaps most notably that of personnel management, the situation was rather different. In only a few pre-1974 NHS authorities had personnel management developed as a specialism within administration; very few NHS officers held a qualification in personnel management. Yet now each region or area was to appoint a regional or area personnel officer.

It was also proposed that there should be district personnel officers. The desire of the staff organisations to confine competition for these, as well as other posts, to serving NHS officers meant there would be an acute shortage of qualified candidates, and in the event many appointments were made of officers with no particularly relevant experience, who had to acquire the necessary skills as they went along. Thus the personnel function in the reorganised NHS got off to a bad start.

The Staff Commission arranged that those officers who wished to be considered for top posts in the new service would list on one application form up to five posts of the same type, in order of preference. The area posts were dealt with first and short lists for all ninety authorities were drawn up by the Staff Commission with the help of panels of assessors from the various professions and from outside the NHS. Interviews were then conducted by the authorities themselves, with the help of assessors nominated by the Staff Commission. The choice of assessors posed some problems, as they had to be people who were not themselves competing for posts. Most were therefore retired or on the point of retirement. Some were inferior in rank to those they were interviewing.

The first short lists to be drawn up were those for posts as area administrator, area nursing officer and area treasurer. Because officers were notified individually, and letters to candidates who had not been short-listed went out a week later than those to officers who had, there was some delay before people compared notes and rumbles of discontent started to be heard. The picture that emerged was one in which rationality appeared to have been discarded. It was impossible to identify any consistent set of criteria which the Staff Commission might have been using when they drew up the short lists. Top-graded group secretaries and chief nursing officers were stunned to learn they had not been short-listed for any of the five posts for which they had applied, while others, considerably less well qualified and experienced, had been more fortunate. Officers who had not been short-listed for their 'own' area posts (some areas corresponded closely to the catchment areas of existing hospital groups) found they had been short-listed for jobs carrying considerably higher salaries. One senior administrator, who had no personal complaint because he had been short-listed for all the posts for which he had applied, said: 'There is no way of telling what criteria these fools are using. There are too many contradictions. The damage that has been done in the past week is irreparable. It will leave its mark on morale for the next twenty years.' In the House of Lords, Lord Reigate told the government that senior staff in the NHS were 'disillusioned with those in command. They are uncertain as to what has happened and who has blundered. They are uncertain as to where they are all heading.'

Still the Staff Commission floundered on, producing other short lists which caused further waves of indignation and bewilderment, and reiterating their confidence in the panels of assessors and in the procedures which had been followed. Only the fact that many authorities failed to make appointments after the first round of interviews created the opportunity for further short lists to be prepared and for some of the earlier mistakes to be rectified without the Staff Commission losing face. For the second round of interviews the Staff Commission wisely allowed the authorities themselves to prepare the short lists, and indeed there are grounds for believing that some authorities failed to appoint on the first occasion so as to be able to insist that they be allowed to consider a particular candidate whom the Staff Commission had excluded.

OTHER DIFFICULTIES

Apart from the activities of the Staff Commission, morale was also affected unhappily by the dealings of the department over the pay of senior staff. Before the Appointed Day, local government staff were given extra payments for the additional work that reorganisation entailed; their colleagues from the hospital service who worked with them on JLCs were denied any such payment. There were delays in fixing the salaries attaching to the top posts with the new authorities and there was discontent when it was discovered that equal status as members of management teams did not mean equal pay. Administrators and treasurers were paid less than the doctors, and the nurses were paid least of all. Negotiations having failed, the salaries of a number of posts had to be promulgated unilaterally by the secretary of state.

Some of the difficulties, and the consequent damage to morale, could be attributed to the tempo at which it was necessary for matters to proceed if the deadline of reorganisation on 1 April 1974 were to be met. The government refused to consider any postponement, regarding it as vital that local government and the NHS should be reorganised on the same day. A steady stream of paper poured out of the DHSS, refining and developing earlier guidance and creating the impression of a central department determined to control every detail, but hardly able to co-ordinate the work of its own divisions. Courses were organised at national and regional centres to brief staff on the principles of the reorganised NHS and to introduce them, *inter alia*, to the delights of the new and formidably documented NHS planning system. By this time many senior officers and members of authorities were discovering unexpected virtues in the existing structure of the service and wondering whether structural reorganisation would in fact prove the answer to the problems it was designed to solve. By this time, however, reorganisation had an inexorable momentum of its own, as the Labour government who came to power in February 1974 discovered when they wondered whether it was too late to do anything about aspects of the new structure which they disliked. They quickly concluded that it would be irresponsible and impracticable to make major changes at so late a date.

Thus it was in an uncertain atmosphere that the new authorities took over responsibility for the health service. On the Appointed Day itself the majority of staff went about their accustomed duties and few patients had any reason to notice that anything out of the ordinary had happened. That is not to say that the demoralisation of senior staff had no effects further down the line. It was inevitable that middle managers should feel uneasy when they observed the experience of their chiefs. However, it rapidly became impossible to identify separately the effects of reorganisation from the repercussions of the economic crisis into which the country was plunging. It may be that if the service had not found itself short of money and if resources had been available to finance continued expansion, things would soon have settled down. Or it may be that if the staff had been in good heart and if the ranks of senior and experienced administrators had not been heavily depleted by the unexpectedly high proportion who had chosen early retirement rather than compete for jobs on the Staff Commission's terms, the difficulties would have been faced as difficulties had been faced before, with resolution and a sense of dedication to the service and the interests of patients. As it was, the reorganised NIIS could hardly have got off to a worse start. And still the paper flowed in torrents from the DHSS.

10
What's Past is Prologue – an Assessment

In such a large governmental office as the Count's, it may occasionally happen that one department ordains this, another that; neither knows of the other, and though the supreme control is absolutely efficient, it comes by its nature too late, and so every now and then a trifling miscalculation arises.

Franz Kafka, *The Castle*

The time has come to sum up, to consider to what degree the National Health Service in its first twenty-six years realised the hopes of its founders, and with what prospects did it face the future as it lay mauled and bleeding under the surgeon's knife in April 1974. More than three years have now passed and new patterns are emerging, but they are patterns moulded by the past, as indeed the NHS in its first years was moulded by its inheritance from former times. In attempting an assessment we must beg some questions. For example, who, apart from Aneurin Bevan and his Cabinet colleagues, had a claim to be considered among the founders of the NHS? Except in so far as it is answered in Chapter 1 that question will not be pursued here. It seems fair, however, to assume that all those who gave Bevan and the idea of a national health service their support hoped that new arrangements for the administration and financing of health services in Britain would ensure a greater improvement in the health of the British people than would occur if existing arrangements were allowed to continue, and to develop along lines which had been evident before the war.

Looking back, it is extremely difficult to find any evidence that this has been the case. When Aesop's fly settled on the axle of the moving cart, he looked back and cried: 'What a great dust I raise!' Similarly, politicians and administrators have been prone to claim for the National Health Service credit for such demonstrable improvements in the health of the British people as have occurred since 1948. But is it reasonable to suppose that had the State not taken over financial and administrative responsibility for the health services, and if the hospitals had not been nationalised, the British people would have been denied the benefits of medical progress or that some improvement in health would not have been evident from rising standards of living generally? Surely not. But let us examine the evidence.

THE HEALTH OF THE PEOPLE

It has already been pointed out, in Chapter 1, that while the crude death rate had fallen, in 1938, the last full year of peace, to 11·6 per 1,000 population, it was still 11·6 at the beginning of the 1970s, although there had in fact been some small improvement, which is revealed if the figures are standardised for age and sex. None the less there was no dramatic fall in overall mortality. On the other hand, by 1948 the scope for further improvement was clearly more limited than it had been at the beginning of the century.

The fall in the infant death rate from 53 per 1,000 live births (England and Wales) just before the war to 17·5 in the early 1970s has the appearance of a creditable achievement, but international comparisons gave no grounds for complacency. (If the Scottish figures were brought into the calculation they gave even less.) The Swedish rate was 11·0, the Dutch – with a high proportion of home deliveries and no national health service – was 12·7, and in the period under review England and Wales slipped from fifth to eighth place (Scotland from eighth to twelfth) in the international league table.

Looking back to the time when the Guillebaud Committee were expressing concern about the state of the maternity services, we can now see that the stillbirth rate, which had been falling until the introduction of the NHS, had flattened out, and there was no further improvement until after 1958. This hiccough in a falling graph has been persuasively attributed to changes in the utilisation of services brought about by the NHS. After 1948 mothers tended to make less use of the local authority clinics, and turned increasingly to general practitioners and hospital maternity departments for antenatal care.

The conquest of tuberculosis and other infectious diseases, and the consequent reduction in mortality in the middle years of life, stemmed from the introduction of antibiotics and techniques of immunisation that were being developed before 1948, and these are advances in which all developed countries have shared, irrespective of how they organise or finance their health services. And if it is impossible to make out a convincing case for the NHS on the basis of mortality statistics, it is even more difficult to do so on the basis of such indicators of morbidity – illness or disability not resulting in death – as are available to us. The naïvety of early hopes that the NHS, by reducing morbidity in the working population, would pay for itself through improvements in productivity, was underlined by the steady rise, throughout the period, in days of work lost through sickness. We now understand what was not clearly understood in 1948, that health is a relative matter, and that a decision to go off sick has as much to do with economic as medical factors. An improvement in the general standard of health may lead a worker to take more seriously an ailment which he would at an earlier time have regarded as trivial, and a worker who is able to subsist while off sick on social security payments will more readily take sick leave than one whose income ceases as soon as he stops work. More intangible factors concerned with attitudes and commitment to work may also enter into the decision and thus ultimately influence the statistics. When looking at statistics of absence through sickness we are therefore left with a set of figures which tell us little, if anything, about the performance of the NHS.

The same is true of other changes, both for the better and for the worse. Just as in earlier times, standards of nutrition, housing and of living generally influenced the health of the population as powerfully as, and at times more powerfully than, the health services provided, so may some of the indicators of the changing health of the population between 1948 and 1974 be susceptible of this type of explanation. However, when people have the opportunity to eat more, and spend more, they do not necessarily eat wisely, or spend wisely, and while an increase in average height probably reflects nutritional improvement, the increased incidence of ischaemic heart disease during the same period may reflect dietary habits that have changed in some respects for the worse, and the increase in deaths from cancer of the lung is the price that has to be paid for the smoking of cigarettes.

ACCESS TO HEALTH CARE

Evidence that health, and indeed mortality, is related at least as much to economic and social factors as to the medical services which are available is offered by the remarkably persistent differences between social classes which have provided a focus for radical criticism of the NHS. While it can be accepted that to make the full range of health services equally available to all groups in the community was an object very much in the minds of the founders of the NHS, the sweeping away of financial barriers has apparently not been enough for modern critics. Yet only if health services could be shown to be a crucial factor in differences in health and mortality between different social classes would there be a legitimate ground for criticism of the NHS in the existence of such differences.

There is no dispute that the differences exist. It is indeed striking that in the 1970s the gap between the upper and lower social classes in terms of mortality experience was two to three times as large as in the early 1930s. Most major causes of death are now two or three times as common among social classes IV and V as among classes I and II, and the overall death rate was by the early 1970s 50 per cent higher among the lower than among the upper classes. This disparity appeared to be related to income, to have very little to do with the medical services available, and to be derived largely from differences in diet. Differences between the social classes go beyond mortality and extend also to morbidity, but what seems to matter is not what standard of medical care a patient receives when he is sick, but whether he gets a killing disease to start with. However, in 1972 the General Household Survey, comparing unskilled with professional men and women, found that in England and Wales nearly three times as many unskilled men, and more than three times as many unskilled women, suffered from long-standing illness, disability or infirmity.

There is equally no dispute that there are wide differences in the level of NHS spending in different regions and different localities and that these are such as to have given rise to the promulgation of the 'inverse care law' that the quality of health services varies inversely with the need for them. What is lacking, however, is any firm evidence that greater expenditure on health services would do much for the health of communities which suffer from poverty, bad housing, under-nutrition, and in all likelihood the prevalence of a variety of inherited defects.

The problems faced by the NHS in any attempt to make services available on the basis of need are illustrated by the limited success of measures designed to improve the distribution of general practitioners. In industrial areas, general practitioners tend to have larger lists than elsewhere, and middle-class patients tend to be on small lists or on the lists of practitioners with further qualifications. The system of declaring certain areas to be over-doctored and of offering financial incentives to doctors to work where they were most needed had little success in altering the distribution of general practitioners. There are some areas so inherently unattractive to a professional man – and his family – that no feasible set of financial incentives will persuade him to work in them, and there are others where competition for practices and posts is likely always to be intense. As it is not within the power of the NHS to alter the social structure or indeed the social and economic geography, of the country, only limited blame can be attached to the service for such failures.

Concern with geographical inequalities led to the appointment in 1975 of a Resource Allocation Working Party to see whether the new NHS could not be more successful than the old in overcoming 'the inertia built into the system by history'. The working party's report (the RAWP Report), published in 1976, proposed a formula to relate financial allocations to need and suggested that such traditionally well-financed regions as the four Thames regions and Oxford should be held back while others, such as the North Western, Trent and Northern regions, who traditionally had been allocated rather less than the formula suggested they should have, were allowed to catch up.

The RAWP Report was greeted with dismay by the threatened regions and jubilation by those to whom it offered more. It was attacked for using mortality statistics as indicators of need, but statistics for morbidity were so incomplete and unreliable that mortality ratios had been used as a proxy for morbidity. The working party suggested that the formula should not only be used as a basis of allocation to regions, but by regions as a basis for allocation of funds to areas. There seemed to be built in to the RAWP recommendations an assumption that two authorities, and two teams of officers, given equal resources, would necessarily provide an equal volume of services, of equal quality. This assumption made no allowance for wide variations in ability, judgement and commitment, nor did it take account of the fact that regions deprived in other ways were also likely to have more than their fair share of below-average doctors, administrators and nurses.

Inequalities of provision reflected not only social class and geography, but also disease category. As was pointed out in Chapter 5, there were wide disparities in cost between acute and long-stay hospitals, between hospitals for the physically and the mentally ill, and these disparities could not be accounted for by the more costly treatments required for acute physical illnesses, but also extended to such things as food and domestic services. From the 1960s onwards, successive ministers and secretaries of state expressed their concern, and declared their determination to improve the lot of patients in the long-stay sector. Again, renewed efforts were made in the early years after reorganisation, and in 1976 the DHSS produced a Consultative Document on Priorities for Health and Personal Social Services in England, which reiterated earlier statements about the importance of prevention, the need to give priority to the mentally ill and the mentally handicapped, as well as the aged, and the need to shift emphasis from hospitals to services in the community.

However, a check on the department's record in translating such good intentions into action shows that, for instance, publication in 1971 of *Better Services for the Mentally Handicapped*, which called for a certain amount of new building, was followed by a fall in the proportion of NHS capital expenditure devoted to this class of patient from 5·4 per cent in the year of publication to 3·7 per cent in 1974/5; and in spite of numerous official pronouncements during the 1960s, the proportion of NHS revenue expenditure devoted to services for the mentally ill actually fell from 12·9 per cent in 1964/5 to 11·26 per cent in 1973/4. Similar failures to translate policy into action had occurred in the field of local authority social services designed to complement and relieve the pressure on NHS provision, and in the field of preventive services.

What is in question here is not the sincerity of Ministers or the DHSS, nor the desirability or otherwise of the policies mentioned, but the feasibility of exercising on a national basis the kind of detailed control necessary to give full effect to them. A high proportion of NHS costs are accounted for by staff wages and salaries, and the level of these is only partly within the control of the DHSS. An unusually generous pay award to a particular group of staff can have a considerable distorting effect on patterns of expenditure. The limited extent to which it is possible to redeploy staff, and to retrain them for other work, is a further limiting factor to the ability of the DHSS to bring about a shift of resources to deprived areas or specialities. Other constraints include such residual autonomy as remains with the subordinate health authorities, and perhaps even more importantly the degree of autonomy traditionally, and probably rightly, accorded the medical profession in the treatment and care of patients.

Thus equality of access, and equality of facilities for different social classes, geographical areas and disease categories, while undoubtedly reflecting, as objectives, the ideals of the party and the government that brought the NHS into being, have proved more difficult of realisation than might have been imagined in the early days; and the experience of the first twenty-six years must surely raise the question as to whether such equality might not be a mirage, that draws the traveller on, and then, as he seems to be in striking distance of it, disappears, only to manifest itself once more in the far distance, and exert once again its fatal lure, until in the end the traveller falls, exhausted, but dimly conscious that he might have used his efforts in some more profitable enterprise.

THE NATIONAL HEALTH SERVICE AND THE ECONOMY

We have already cast doubt on the extent to which the NHS can be regarded as an economic asset, in the sense of contributing directly to a more productive workforce. Perhaps it could have been more of an asset than it has been. An ordering of priorities which directed resources to reducing the waiting-lists for the treatment of such disabling conditions as hernia, or to the more effective treatment and rehabilitation of cases of accidental injury, might have helped to offset some of the other factors which have tended to produce rising sickness-absence rates, but there is no guarantee that such priorities, even if selected by ministers, would have proved any easier to translate into action than those which were selected. A change in the financial basis of the NHS would probably be required to ensure that such economically attractive policies were in fact pursued.

If the NHS represents, to a large extent, consumption rather than investment, is it possible to go further, and argue that the NHS has imposed burdens on the economy that might have been avoided had some other system of organising and financing health services been chosen, or allowed to evolve, after the war? The reorganised NHS faces many problems, all of which have been exacerbated by the unprecedented decline in the British economy in the last decade. It is worth emphasising that although recession has been worldwide, no other major economy has experienced so severe a crisis, so severe a failure to achieve every economic objective, as Britain. If the NHS has in any way contributed to this decline, then on that score alone it has a formidable case to answer.

The steady absolute and proportional growth in expenditure on the NHS, without any clear evidence of any corresponding economic return, together with the rise in the numbers of staff, some of whom may have been drawn, directly or indirectly, from productive sectors of the economy, creates a prima facie case. The NHS, like certain other non-productive parts of the public sector, finds it easy to offer employment to additional workers in times of recession because as long as money is available to pay their wages it is not necessary to provide, at any rate in the short term, additional buildings or plant to set them to work. These workers seldom return voluntarily to other forms of employment when the economic situation changes, and public sector employment policies (and an assumption that it is a good thing to take the opportunity to expand services and regrettable if they have to be cut back) ensure that their jobs are protected.

This is not the only factor that fosters the secular growth of the NHS and other public service organisations. If we assume that managers and administrators in the NHS are motivated at least to some extent by considerations of advantage to themselves (and to say this is no more than to say that they are human), then it is worth considering what course of action is likely to ensure rewards that will be valued by the manager or administrator, whether these be a higher salary, status and the esteem of colleagues and friends, the opportunity to exercise judgement and responsibility, the opportunity to provide a service that is valued by the community, the opportunity to enjoy autonomy or exercise power, or whatever. By and large a manager in an enterprise that has to market its products, whether these be in the form of goods or services, must have in the forefront of his mind the profitability of the concern, and therefore the satisfaction of market requirements at a price the market is willing to pay, if he hopes to enjoy any of these rewards. In the non-market sector, however (whether it be in public or private hands), the only indicator of performance that is consistently associated with the distribution of valued rewards to senior managers and administrators is a growth in the size and funding of the organisation. Other indicators of performance are frequently non-existent or open to varied interpretations. There is therefore a powerful dynamic of expansion without any corresponding pressures to ensure that expansion is matched by measurable achievement.

In a national health service financed almost entirely from taxation, this expansion has the effect of both increasing the proportion of their wage packets that workers must yield to the State to pay for the NHS and of reducing the resources available to the productive sector. The increased taxation necessary to pay for an expanded health service – and indeed other parts of the public sector that produce goods and services that are not marketed – itself has two effects: (1) diminishing incentives in the productive part of the economy; and (2) diminishing investment in the productive part of the economy. This pattern of a diminishing market sector having increasing difficulty in supporting steadily expanding public services has been at the root of Britain's economic difficulties in the mid-1970s, and it is ironic that workers in the NHS should complain so bitterly at the difficulties created during and after the 1974 reorganisation by the economic situation, when the NHS itself was a major contributing factor. The irony is all the greater in that had the non-market sector not prematurely diverted resources that should have been invested in productive capacity, the consequent expansion of the economy would ultimately have ensured a far larger cake from which the NHS, for example, would have been able to carve a far larger slice, in absolute terms, than has been possible to date, or would appear to be possible in the foreseeable future.

THE NATIONAL HEALTH SERVICE AND THE FUTURE

One of the recurring themes of discussion in the NHS in the years after reorganisation has been 'Which tier will go ?', for there quickly grew up a widespread conviction that the reorganised NHS had one tier too many. The root of the problem was, however, that too many areas had been subdivided into two or more districts that could have been managed as one, and in multi-district areas the area officers, with no authority over their district counterparts, had no proper job of work to do. In single-district areas, with few exceptions, the new structure settled down quickly and people came to terms with their jobs without undue difficulty. More than three years after reorganisation the same cannot be said of the multi-district areas. Tension between area and district officers is common, and it has been estimated that large sums could be saved by merging districts in small to medium-sized authorities, and by splitting the larger authorities into viable single-district areas. In spite of the expressed determination of the DHSS to reduce administrative costs, the likely reaction of staff organisations and interests to any such changes has so far prevented action from being taken and it would appear that resolution of this particular problem will await the report of the Royal Commission on the NHS, which is now sitting.

It seems doubtful whether the advantages hoped for from coterminosity with the new local authorities are in fact being reaped. A statutory duty was laid on both health and local authorities to collaborate and machinery to foster collaboration was set up. Exchequer money was made available for schemes to be jointly financed by health and local authorities. None the less local authorities are frequently not keen to spend ratepayers' money, or commit ratepayers' money in future years, on schemes which NHS authorities consider to be highly desirable.

Management by teams of officers is after three years settling down into an accepted way of life and, in spite of initial bewilderment over the use of the term 'consensus' to describe the prescribed pattern of decision making, is proving to amount to no more than a sensible recognition that the NHS is not a unitary organisation, but a federation of professions and sources of legitimacy and finance which must come together and reconcile their differences if a service is to be provided to the community.

Community health councils may also be accounted one of the successes of reorganisation, although the more successful they are in representing the community, and the more competent the professional managers of the service prove themselves to be, the more likely it is that someone sooner or later will start asking some very pointed questions about the role of authorities and authority members in the reorganised NHS. Deprived of the role in which HMC members could take refuge, that of representing the consumer, AHA members can hardly feel secure in the role of managers in relation to chief officers who are trained and experienced in the management of health services. If it was ever in Sir Keith Joseph's mind that members should be chosen for their managerial ability, that objective was quickly abandoned, and after the 1974 general election successive Labour secretaries of state confused the matter still further by drafting CHC representatives (who none the less had to give up their CHC membership) on to AHAs, and by introducing representatives of the staff working in the area. A chief officer may therefore now have a subordinate, whom it is his duty to direct, appraise and if necessary discipline, as a member of the authority which has it in its remit to direct, appraise and if necessary discipline the chief officers. This Byzantine situation is unhappily typical of the reorganised NHS.

When the first batch of health authority chairmen fell due to have their appointments renewed or terminated in 1977, the secretary of state, David Ennals, failed to renew a number of them, and replaced some with nominees known to be in sympathy with Labour policies and ideals. These appointments were criticised as political patronage (chairmen in the reorganised NHS are paid a part-time salary) and as bringing politics into the NHS. This was hardly realistic; politics cannot be kept out of a service that spends more than £5,000 million of public money each year. However, if in fact authority chairmen are to become political commissars charged with ensuring that the priorities and policies of the government of the day are reflected at local level, there is a certain logic about it and it does give them a coherent role.

In the seven years leading up to NHS reorganisation the numbers of administrative and clerical staff went up by 40 per cent. In the eighteen months following reorganisation, there was a further increase of 20 per cent. Giving evidence to the Public Accounts Committee of the House of Commons in the summer of 1977, Sir Patrick Nairne, permanent secretary at the DHSS, attributed 45 per cent of the increase to the new and more expensive administrative structure, 20 per cent to the new planning system, 15 per cent to improved conditions of service, 10 per cent to work taken over from local authorities and to servicing CHCs, and 10 per cent to improved financial control. However, the cost of the new structure, and of the planning system which like so many aspects of reorganisation appears unlikely to yield the benefits that were hoped for, cannot be reckoned solely in terms of additional administrative and clerical staff employed. Nurses and doctors are also caught up, full-time or part-time, in servicing the new structure or operating the planning system, and so further substantial costs are concealed under these headings. Politically, it is only the identifiable costs of administration that are embarrassing. In the day-to-day administration of services unnecessary complexity of administration is an embarrassment whether it results in identifiable costs or not, and such complexity, with consequent delays in the making of decisions, has been part of the legacy of 1974 with which the NHS now has to contend.

The increased militancy of hospital ancillary staff which led to the strike of 1973 continued after reorganisation, but by then NUPE activities were directed mainly at putting pressure on the government to abolish private beds in NHS hospitals. This pursuit of a political objective through industrial action was an even more novel experience for the NHS than the 1973 strike, but the action eventually taken by the government stopped short of the abolition of private beds in NHS hospitals, and arranged that they should be phased out gradually as alternative facilities became available in wholly private premises. The compromise worked out by Aneurin Bevan had worked well, and probably to the benefit of both private and NHS patients (in so far as consultants treating private patients were working and available on NHS premises and not some distance away in a private hospital), but so pragmatic a solution was considered inappropriate by the NUPE militants, who would have liked the government to come out clearly in favour of abolishing the private practice of medicine altogether. This, however, the government declined to do.

The attack on private medicine aroused an angry response from the consultants, who were also unhappy at the consequences of, first, a pay award achieved by the junior hospital doctors which enabled some of them, by working extensive overtime, to earn more than a consultant, and secondly, government pay policies which denied cost-of-living increases to those already earning more than £8,500 a year. Finally, consultant morale was further depressed by the government's declared intention of shifting resources from hospital to community services and by the financial squeeze on the teaching hospitals, particularly in London.

The picture that has been painted of the NHS in the years immediately after reorganisation would suggest that the only hope for the future is the crumb of comfort that Ian Hay offered the soldiers in his Mudsplosh Camp: 'It can't go on snowing for ever.' On the other hand, it is perhaps more constructive to pin faith in human ability to learn from experience. Just as there is a growing understanding of the roots of Britain's economic problems which may ultimately lead to action that will reverse the downward spiral in her fortunes, so it is to be hoped will certain lessons have been learned from the first twenty-six years of the NHS and from the dismal outcomes of the 1974 reorganisation.

Just as the Guillebaud Committee in the early years of the NHS felt that a period of consolidation was required, so the Royal Commission may suggest that on the whole the service needs a period to settle down after the upheaval of 1974; but even so, some of the difficulties under which the NHS at present labours could be resolved with comparatively little trouble, and if major structural issues cannot be tackled immediately, a further twenty-six years from 1974 would bring us to the turn of the century, and it seems unlikely that so much time will be allowed to elapse before something is done.

The way forward will be one that recognises that the health service has a job to do, a necessary but modest job, and that it will do that job most effectively if it is not at the same time expected to pursue a number of other, often conflicting, aims in the field of social and economic policy. The NHS cannot solve all the problems of society on its own. The service requires flexibility and freedom to respond to the great variety of local circumstances and need that characterise these small but varied islands. Unlimited finance is not one of the requirements. Doctors, nurses and patients alike understand about cutting one's coat according to one's cloth, but the limits on resources are best appreciated, and limited resources are best used, when there is a close association between the raising of money and the spending of it. Above all, the lesson stands out that there is virtue in making haste slowly, in proceeding by trial and error, diversity and experiment, in making small mistakes in order that learning can take place, rather than one large error that must be defended at all costs lest those responsible lose credit. The trend towards over-centralisation and ever-increasing bureaucratic complexity must be reversed, and this will only be achieved if trust is placed in people – people well chosen, well trained and well motivated – rather than in structures and systems.

Further Reading

A number of official and semi-official reports and publications are referred to in the text. Unless otherwise stated, these are published by HM Stationery Office, but a number of the more important documents are outlined and discussed, frequently with extracts, in:

Watkin, B., *Documents on Health and Social Services: 1834 to the Present Day* (London: Methuen, 1975).

The following works discuss the origins and early years of the NHS.

Eckstein, H., *The English Health Service: Its Origins, Structure and Achievements* (Cambridge, Mass.: Harvard University Press, 1959).
Jewkes, J. and Jewkes, Sylvia, *The Genesis of the British National Health Service* (Oxford: Blackwell, 1961).
Lindsey, A., *Socialized Medicine in England and Wales* (Chapel Hill: University of North Carolina Press; and London: OUP, 1962).
Willcocks, A. J., *The Creation of the National Health Service* (London: Routledge & Kegan Paul, 1967).

There is also valuable background in:

Foot, M., *Aneurin Bevan 1945–1960* (London: Davis-Poynter, 1973).
Goodman, N. M., *Wilson Jameson: Architect of National Health* (London: Allen & Unwin, 1970).
Political and Economic Planning, *Report on the British Health Services* (London: PEP, 1937).

Readers interested in the financial problems of the early years should turn to:

Abel-Smith, B. and Titmuss, R. M., *The Cost of the National Health Service in England and Wales* (Cambridge: CUP, 1956).
Roberts, F., *The Cost of Health* (London: Turnstile Press, 1952).

Further material on the medical profession in relation to the NHS will be found in:

Butler, J. R., *Family Doctors and Public Policy* (London: Routledge & Kegan Paul, 1973).
Dopson, L., *The Changing Scene in General Practice* (London: Johnson, 1971).
Forsyth, G., *Doctors and State Medicine* (London: Pitman Medical, 1971).
Goldman, L., *Angry Young Doctor* (London: Hamilton, 1957).
Klein, R., *Complaints Against Doctors* (London: Knight, 1973).

Stevens, Rosemary, *Medical Practice in Modern England* (New Haven: Yale, 1966).

The following reflections by former ministers on their experience of the NHS are valuable.

Crossman, R. H. S., *A Politician's View of Health Service Planning* (Glasgow: The University, 1972).

Owen, D., *In Sickness and in Health: The Politics of Medicine* (London: Quartet Books, 1976).

Powell, J. E., *Medicine and Politics: 1975 and After* (London: Pitman Medical, 1976).

The economic argument in Chapter 10 draws heavily on:

Bacon, R. and Eltis, W., *Britain's Economic Problem: Too Few Producers* (London: Macmillan, 1976).

and also on:

Tullock, G., *The Vote Motive* (London: Institute of Economic Affairs, 1976).

Index